THEY USED TO SAY THAT MARY TYLER MOORE WAS AN ACTRESS WHO ONLY PLAYED HERSELF

That was when she was the star of the joyous hit *The Mary Tyler Moore Show* on TV.

Then that show ended.

Then Mary Tyler Moore appeared in Robert Redford's movie *Ordinary People* as a cold, repressed, perfectionist on the brink of suicide— and it was whispered that *that* was the real Mary Tyler Moore.

Which role mirrored her? And what role does she play now, after so much has happened to dim her smile and shadow her reputation?

Now this probing, compassionate look into the life of Mary Tyler Moore gives you the answers about a star who has won so many fans, and yet has stirred so many questions. . . .

MARY TYLER MOORE: The Woman Behind the Smile

Mary Tyler Moore: The Woman Behind the Smile

AN UNAUTHORIZED BIOGRAPHY

Rebecca Stefoff

AN ULTRA COMMUNICATIONS PRODUCTION

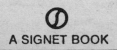

A SIGNET BOOK

NEW AMERICAN LIBRARY

PHOTO INSERT CREDITS

Page 1, top: Courtesy of Pictorial Parade, Inc.; page 1, middle: Courtesy of Pictorial Parade, Inc.; page 1, bottom: Courtesy of Photo Trends; page 2, top: Courtesy of Pictorial Parade, Inc.; page 2, middle: Courtesy of Photo Trends; page 2, bottom: Courtesy of Pictorial Parade, Inc.; page 3, top: © Frank Edwards/ Fotos International; page 3, middle: © Ron Galella; page 3, bottom: © Smeal/Galella; pages 4 and 5, top and bottom: Courtesy of Photo Trends; page 6, top: Courtesy of Photo Trends; page 6, middle: Courtesy of Pictorial Parade, Inc.; page 6, bottom: Courtesy of Photo Trends; page 7, top, middle, and bottom: © Ron Galella; page 8: © Ron Galella

Cover photo courtesy of Outline Press

CONTENTS

Introduction

The smile is her trademark—a quick, broad grin that warms her fine-boned face and crinkles the corners of her huge brown eyes. The smile seems as open and straightforward as the funny, uncomplicated characters who were loved by millions during her hit television years. For more than a quarter of a century, in photo after photo, she has smiled on. Can any woman *really* be that happy? That nice?

Mary Tyler Moore is still smiling, but the smile is now a little wry, a little less assured, and her face is etched with lines of grief as well as laughter. These days, when she smiles, the dark eyes often remain somber. She claims the real Mary is emerging at last.

"I've spent so much of my life smiling, seeking to be liked," she says ruefully. Her smile has often been a barrier to keep others at a distance, a shield held up against the world—even a weapon. In a life filled with dramatic triumphs and tragedies, she's been called every name from "sweet" to "bitchy," and she's earned them all.

What's Mary Tyler Moore really like? Even she doesn't know for sure. But a look behind that famous smile reveals no prime-time Pollyanna. She is a woman more complex, more vital, more troubled, and more fascinating than anyone ever dreamed. Above all, she is a woman of wild, puzzling contradictions.

1

MARY, MARY QUITE CONTRARY

Mary Tyler Moore is a pencil-thin diabetic who gives herself two or more shots of insulin daily yet indulges in uncontrollable, destructive binge eating; a powerful and successful actress who thinks of herself as a failed dancer; an acclaimed natural comedienne who has driven herself to achieve her greatest triumphs in starkly tragic roles. She is a lapsed Catholic who sharply criticizes the Church yet calls her private audience with the pope "the transcendent experience of my life"; a lifelong fitness and exercise addict with a two-and-a-half-pack-a-day cigarette habit; a multi-millionaire celebrity who feels inferior because she didn't go to college; a New York–California hybrid, a city girl whose most memorable roles have been as suburban or midwestern women.

Esquire magazine fondly hailed her as "America's Sweetheart," but some other members of the press dubbed her "the Ice Princess" for her cold, reserved personality. She split with her husband of seventeen years just weeks after saying she'd be lost without him. She married her third husband, sixteen years her junior, just weeks after vowing she'd never marry again. She has yearned for order, discipline, and control to be her ruling passions yet recently sought treatment for alcoholism.

She became famous playing squeaky-clean women whose biggest problems were dented fenders or eccentric coworkers, but her own life has been as full of tragedy as any long-running soap opera. She has endured a troubled relationship with her parents, a teenage marriage to get away from home, two divorces, a near-fatal miscarriage, serious bouts with an incurable disease, several humiliating and highly publicized stage and screen flops, the suicide of her younger sister, and the death of her only child from a self-inflicted gunshot. Clearly, smiling hasn't always been easy for Mary Tyler Moore.

"Couldn't you just slap my face for being so positive and optimistic?" she asked an interviewer from the Sunday *New York Times Magazine* in 1974. While the remark playfully acknowledges her wholesome, Goody Two-Shoes image, it also hints at another side of her character: a self-mocking irony that Mary has kept under wraps most of the time. At the heart of all the contradictions in Mary's life are two powerful, opposing drives.

On one hand, she's a relentless perfectionist who disciplines every minute of her life. "I'm such a planner, I'd plan a headache if I could," she says, only half joking. On the other hand, she sometimes reveals "a part of me that wants to let go, to thumb my nose at the rest of the world." Because of the control she exerts over herself most of the time, Mary has found it hard to thumb her nose at the world in ordinary, harmless ways. Instead, she eats or drinks too much, makes herself sick, or cries "full-out, racking sobs" in private.

For the first twenty years of her career, Mary's public image of perky, always-smiling ordinariness was carefully crafted and maintained—by Mary herself, by her publicists and writers, and by her second husband, Grant Tinker, who catapulted Mary to fame. Tinker himself is an enigmatic man who seldom indulges in personal interviews. He has usually been viewed as a powerful, though benevolent, Svengali-like mentor who shaped Mary's career and made her decisions until she outgrew him. Her own contradictory statements sometimes confirm, sometimes deny this interpretation of their relationship. It's clear, though, that he was the prime mover in making her a superstar and a superpower in the entertainment industry.

At the same time, Mary was gradually acquiring a somewhat different image within the entertainment world. She gained a reputation as a shrewd, hard-headed businesswoman who knew how to take care of herself and her career, and who exerted strict control over interviews and publicity. In an industry noted for its compulsive socializing, she and Grant Tinker led quiet, intensely private lives. So reserved was Mary in her professional contacts that some colleagues and observers called her cold, rigid, and impersonal—Ed Asner, who was Mary's on-screen mentor, father figure, and boss for seven years, has said that on a personal level Mary Tyler Moore is "a closed corporation," something she shared with the stunning character she created in *Ordinary People*. Others, perhaps responding more to the qualities Mary drew on for her portrayals of Laura Petrie and Mary Richards on television, found her honest, funny, and friendly.

But despite these contradictory opinions about her personality, Mary always appeared contented, confident, and in control. She was the best possible all-American girl next door: bright, funny, innocently sexy, always a good girl—on camera and off. Only in the 1980s, after divorcing Tinker and moving from Hollywood to New York, did she begin to reveal the cracks in that glossy picture of the idyllic childhood, the perfect marriage, the well-managed life.

Today it seems as if Mary is working overtime to dispel her earlier image. Indeed, it's hard to imagine the old Mary, America's sweetheart, inviting Betty White and Gavin MacLeod and the rest of *The Mary Tyler Moore Show* gang to a private screening of *Ordinary People*, only to stride into the room—late—in a parachutist's jump suit and exclaim, "Let's start this mother!"

And it's downright impossible to imagine Laura Petrie or Mary Richards checking into the Betty Ford Center for alcoholism treatment. But, says Mary, "I'm learning that it's okay to be ugly, to have a pimple, to let my hair down. I'm doing the things I *want* to do, not what I should do. It's essential that I make my own decisions."

Some of those decisions have obviously been good ones. In the past few years, she has succeeded in a string of television, stage and screen roles that crushed the Pollyanna image before returning to the medium for which she is still best known, TV comedy. In the wake of a series of crippling personal losses, she coped with living on her own for the first time—and in the process made some unexpected discoveries. And although some of her friends were extremely critical of her third—and most unconventional—marriage, she recently celebrated its second anniversary and claims to be as much in love as ever.

Along the way, Mary has opened up a little, to the public and to the people in her life. After years of formal, polished interviews which were explicitly limited to professional or harmless questions ("How do you create your characters, Miss Moore?" and "What are your hobbies, Miss Moore?"), Mary kicked off the Eighties with a flurry of more candid, personal interviews in magazines and newspapers. She apparently felt that the new life she was building in the wake of her second divorce, the death of her son, and her relocation to New York called for a looser, less rigidly private image. She began seeing a therapist, and she openly discussed some of the problems she tried to overcome, such as her dependence on dominant men and learning how to be alone.

However she hasn't done a complete turnabout. There are still plenty of topics that are off limits. She refuses to answer probing questions about her relationship with her parents, for example, or either of her divorces, as she feels that would violate the privacy of people other than herself. But on the whole, she is now more accessible and revealing to the public.

Mary has also made herself more available to friends. Years ago, in a surprisingly gruesome but characteristic figure of speech that hints at the black humor just beneath Mary's smiling surface, she told an interviewer, "If I had to spend as much time talking to a friend about myself as I'm spending with you, I'd open a vein, it would be that uncomfortable for me!" And she says rather sadly of her many years in California with Tinker, "He wasn't just my best friend—he was my only friend." Although she had good relationships with many women, including such colleagues as Betty White and Valerie Harper, Mary came to feel that all her friendships were rather superficial.

She blames herself for that. With the new insight that she began to develop after the move to New York, she says, "For the longest time I would share only my 'up' moments with my friends. I felt that to let them into my problems, the dreary parts of my life, would be a burden. I never saw before that it wasn't fair to friends to present myself as a person without problems; I didn't understand that it was depriving *them* of a chance to be human." So Mary Tyler Moore is now admitting that she—like everybody else—has problems.

"I've broken out of a shell," she says. "I'm looking at myself, rather than just smiling through life, denying emotions I've been afraid of. I did not want to go on being closed to myself, pretending, acting things out, having acquaintances instead of friends. Oh, this sounds so boring, but I'm finding out who I am."

And she's letting others begin to find out, too.

2

FROM BROOKLYN BABY TO Hollywood Hoofer

Mary Tyler Moore was a holiday baby, born between Christmas and New Year's on December 29, 1937. If her parents had been given to astrological musing, they might have wondered whether their firstborn child would grow up to be a typical Capricorn, who is said to be financially shrewd, a good money-maker, but who can appear cold and unemotional. Most likely, however, the Moores were too practical and hardheaded for such fanciful speculation.

Mary's background was comfortably middle-class— exactly the sort of background that might have produced Mary Richards, except that it was set on the East Coast instead of in the Midwest. She still remembers the address where she was born and lived for her first few years: 491 Ocean Parkway in Brooklyn. The family next lived in Flushing for several years, then moved back to Brooklyn, where Mary attended St. Rose of Lima Grammar School.

George Tyler Moore, Mary's father, was a goodlooking, bookish Irish-American—and a strict Catholic, a fact that had a powerful impact on young

Mary. Her mother, Marjorie Hackett Moore, came
from a Protestant background but agreed to raise
their children in the Catholic Church. Although he
had graduated *magna cum laude* from Georgetown
University, George Moore held an unimpressive job
in a utility company when Mary was born.

Because Mary has been ambitious since childhood,
she never understood her father's lack of ambition.
"Absolutely no career drive," she said of him. "I
can't account for that. He was an enigma to me. I
won't say cold, but reserved. He's an intellectual, a
buttoned-up man who cared nothing for show business and had a hard time communicating any affection
for me." But she's aware that her uneasy relationship with her father provided at least part of the
energy that propelled her to stardom.

"I think a lot of my career drive is based on a
childhood need to get Daddy's approval and attention," Mary admits. "So if I *had* had that wonderful,
perfect, loving relationship with my father that everybody craves, I might not have the gumption to do
what I do now—to put myself on the line. I guess it's
too bad we didn't have a close, loving relationship, but
who's to say? Maybe not. I like what I am, I love
what I do—and he formed me." He formed more
aspects of Mary than her show-business ambition,
though. Her ambivalent relationship with him also
formed a pattern in her relationships with men and
her marriage partners, a pattern that she was not to
break until her own middle age.

But Mary's serious problems with her parents were
still far in the future during the early Brooklyn years.
World War II began when Mary was barely two, and

the United States entered the war almost on her fourth birthday. But her clearest memory of the turbulent war years is of the morale-boosting, patriotic musicals that flooded the movie theaters of America. She adored the dancers. And when Mary played dress-up, she didn't pretend to be Mommy waiting for Daddy to come home from work—no, she pretended to be Ginger Rogers, being swept off her dancing feet by Fred Astaire.

Tap and ballet lessons were all the rage for budding Shirley Temples, and Mary was no exception. Her mother signed her up for ballet, and she was hooked from the moment she took her first step. Her mother remembers Mary asking every day to be driven to the studio so she could practice "for just one more hour." Marjorie Moore adds that at times Mary was "a pain in the neck, because she wanted to be a dancer and actress so badly." Mary herself has memories that might have come right out of a Mickey Rooney–Judy Garland movie: "My cousins and I constantly put on shows. I was *frantic* to be a performer!"

But unlike most of the little ballerinas in Brooklyn, Mary really had a connection to show business—on her mother's side of the family. Her uncle, Harold Hackett, lived in Los Angeles, where he was a vicepresident of MCA. (He later became president of Official Films, which produced *Robin Hood* for television.) He sang the praises of the Southern California climate and, during his visits to the Moores and in letters, regaled them with heady tales of playing golf with Bob Hope.

George Tyler Moore may not have been star-struck, but he did decide to move the family to California.

When Mary was eight, he got a job with the South-
ern California Gas Company, and Mary found her-
self living in the land of her dreams, Hollywood.
Mary's aunt, her mother's sister, Bertie Hackett, also
went west with the Moores. She left NBC radio in
New York to become business manager of station
KNXT in Los Angeles. Having settled there, the
Moores stayed put; Mary's parents still live in Studio
City, a Hollywood suburb.

In her new home, Mary attended Catholic schools
that she later described as "very strict": St. Ambrose
Grammar School and Immaculate Heart High School.
Her school years were notable only in negative ways.
For one thing, her grades were terrible, which disap-
pointed her father. "I was a lousy high-school student," she admits. "Lousy."

Another growing problem was her rebellion against
the strict discipline of the nuns. Two incidents in
particular stand out in her memory. "I had a lot of
guilt as a child that goes back to going to my first
confession," she says. "I was found talking in line by
the sister in charge, and sent over to the boys' line. I
was so humiliated. And I remember playing basket-
ball in the school yard several years later. The girls
had one area of the yard, the boys another. I was
playing with the boys. A sister came over and said,
'Come here, young lady. Don't you EVER do that.
You're not allowed to play with boys.' I had to stay
after school. These are little scars but you carry them
with you."

Mary's uneasy relationship with the Church was
further eroded a few years later when she confessed
to making out with a boy. Told that prolonged kiss-

ing was a sin, she said to herself, "Well, we have a bit of a problem here, because I intend to go on engaging in prolonged kissing." As time went on, Mary's increasing disregard for the strictures of the Church would be echoed by a growing rebelliousness at home.

Yet her childhood love of show business never wavered—in fact, it grew stronger by the day. Mary had little time for homework or extracurricular activities, but she became a movie junkie. She loved both Hepburns, Cyd Charisse, and especially Leslie Caron. "Caron had all those *teeth*," she says, "and I was so self-conscious about my big mouth. But there she was, *adored* for her big mouth, plus she was a brilliant dancer. I wanted to be just like her. And she was dancing with *my* Gene Kelly, my idol. God, I *hated* her!"

Movies notwithstanding, Mary's chief passion was still dancing. Soon after moving to Los Angeles, her mother had enrolled her in the prestigious Ward Sisters Studio of Dance Arts. She may have skimped on schoolwork, but Mary lived for her dance classes and practice sessions. Nothing else mattered, after all. She was going to be a dancer! Looking back on her obsessive single-mindedness, Mary now has some regrets: "It's a shame, because it kept me from being curious about anything else." Focusing all of her impressive energy and intelligence on dance from early childhood, Mary did poorly in school and had no interest in college. As a result, she grew up with a deep sense of intellectual inferiority that haunted her for years.

That feeling of inferiority was to be compounded

by another failure, even harder to bear: Mary would never make it as a dancer. Early in her career, she made the wise decision to shift from dancing to acting, but she never outgrew the desire to excel as a dancer. Her attempts to do so led to several serious professional disasters. And at the pinnacle of her acting success, she confessed, "I will go to my grave thinking of myself as a failed dancer," in much the way that an anorectic woman sees only the ghost of her formerly fat body in the mirror, never her truly thin self.

In typically self-critical fashion, Mary blames her own completely normal instincts for her failure. "I was good," she says. "And I knew I wanted to be a dancer. But I didn't pursue my training with complete devotion—I kept falling in love! I wanted boyfriends and dates. I wasn't cut out for the ascetic life of a dancer—I failed, as everybody's been good enough to remind me. But dancing is my first love and always will be."

Teenage hormones aren't the whole story, however. The quality of her life at home was deteriorating. She had a younger brother now, John, born when she was eight. He is a curiously shadowy figure in Mary's life, never mentioned in interviews or articles. Because she had already discovered the passion for dance that was to consume all of her time from then on, little Mary had in some ways done much of her growing up by the time John was born, and it's understandable that the two didn't have much in common or become close.

Nor was Mary close to her parents. "I can't really put my finger on why that was," she says. "It might have been as simple as teenage rebellion." Or it might have been that Mary's show-business aspirations were a source of friction, especially between her and her father. Because both she and her father were reserved and intensely private, communication between them was difficult, if not impossible.

There were long periods when Mary and her parents just didn't communicate, yet she didn't feel alone in the world. "I want to speak about the virtues of an extended family," she says. "My relatives were always there when I needed them." She spent many childhood weekends at the nearby home of her Aunt Bertie and her maternal grandmother, who was English, and whom Mary describes as "very much a lady, and warm and loving." So it seemed natural, when things at home got too tense, for Mary to move in with the two Hackett women from time to time. She lived with them for two extended periods during high school (and she would return to them during her first big personal crisis some years later). "There was no acrimonious parting from my parents—I saw them on weekends—so there didn't have to be a dramatic reconciliation scene," she says, instinctively replaying her life in theatrical terms.

Mary has always been reticent about her personal relationships, not only because of her own love of privacy, but also because she respects the privacy owed to other people's intimate business. So details about her difficulties with her parents are scant. "There are things I could say for print that would explain everything, but in my mind and in my heart those would be indictments of my parents I don't want to make. I believe they did the best they could at the

Rebecca Stefoff

time in raising me. I didn't see it, and I wanted to live elsewhere. Sure, I think I was being a rotten kid, but there were parts of what they did in raising me that were a little rotten, too." She concludes, "I didn't like them very much, and I really wanted to be independent."

Mary's extended family proved to be more than just a haven from her troubles at home. Her grandmother and aunt encouraged her show-business dreams, but it was her uncle who really tried to help her make them come true. "In high school I'd go see agents with letters from Uncle Harold and tell them I'd studied dancing," she recalls. "They wanted to help and were very nice, but they had no way of knowing whether what they were looking at had any talent." Uncle Harold's letters were slow to open the magic door to stardom, so Mary had to look elsewhere for a key to the independence she craved.

She found it in a most unexpected place.

3

The Only Way Out— and Up

"I wanted to get out of my parents' house," Mary says. "Back then, marriage was the only way out, if you didn't want to go to college."

Marriage hadn't figured in Mary's career plans. But when her career failed to materialize overnight and her desire to get away from her parents and live her own life increased, it was natural for her to consider her options. After all, in the 1950s young girls simply didn't live on their own. And even the most ambitious of them wanted husbands, too.

Mary hadn't had close friendships as a girl. She was always busy with her dancing, for one thing. For another, she was noted for her good behavior in school, despite her bad grades. She simply wasn't the popular or gregarious type. But she did have a healthy interest in boys and she did date. She even dated the Boy Next Door.

There were, however, several significant departures from the old cliché. For one thing, Richard Carlton Meeker didn't really live next door—he simply lived in Mary's parents' neighborhood. Even more important, though, he wasn't a boy—he was the Man

Next Door. Mary met him when she was seventeen and he was twenty-seven. Ten years isn't an insuperable obstacle to a successful relationship, by any means. But the decade between the teens and the late twenties is an important one in terms of arriving at maturity. And while the difference between, say, forty-five and fifty-five may be negligible, ten years is a big chunk of a seventeen-year-old's life.

Perhaps Mary was attracted by the very fact that Richard was so much older, already out on his own and apparently ready to offer that same freedom to her. She has always been guarded in her references to him and to their marriage, but admits that she fell in love with him quickly, even impetuously.

Ironically, it was Mary's mother who fixed them up. Meeker, who has been variously described as a food broker and a CBS sales executive, met Marjorie Moore in early 1955 while both were running errands in the neighborhood. He lived in an apartment building near the Moores' house. Marjorie liked Richard, and encouraged her daughter to meet him. Mary agreed, and the two began to date. After they'd been dating seriously for a while, Richard proposed. And Mary accepted.

"Why did I do it?" she says. "I guess out of a need to assert my individuality—and I foolishly thought that the only option for me was to marry. I'm a part-foolish person. Always will be. Anyway, that's what girls did if they didn't go to college, isn't it? I wanted my own apartment; I wanted to be independent of my folks; I wanted to put myself in a situation where no one could tell me what to do."

Another reason Mary was eager to jump into marriage may have been the same reason she parted with the Church—her normal interest in sex, which had been a source of conflict with her religious background ever since she confessed to kissing a boy. "Marriage was the natural progression for all healthy people who didn't become nuns," she says wryly. "But at the time I certainly believed that I was in love and was going to have a perfect little marriage.

"I was a very good Catholic girl," she continues. "I was a virgin when I married, but I knew when I was dating that there were too many restrictions placed on you, too many sexual taboos."

Mary's marriage signaled her formal break with Catholicism—but certainly not the end of her religious convictions. "I still pray," she says. "I still give thanks, but I do believe that on my deathbed I would not call for a priest. I can't go along with the Church on birth control, divorce, abortion. If I had the choice, I would choose not to be raised a Catholic."

More than just plans for marriage were filling Mary's life in the spring of 1955. After all her unproductive interviews with agents and casting directors, she got her first big break as her senior year of high school drew to a close. She was signed to do a television commercial. She left her senior prom at nine P.M. —with no regrets—to be ready for her first film session the following day. She and Richard were married barely a month later.

The commercial was for Hotpoint appliances, sponsors of *The Adventures of Ozzie and Harriet*, and Mary was cast as Happy Hotpoint, a pixie reduced by camera tricks to three inches in height who danced on top of a Hotpoint stove. She didn't have much trouble memorizing the script; her one line was, "Hi, Harriet, aren't you glad you bought a Hotpoint?" She had more trouble, though, fitting the image of a sexless little elf. At five feet six inches and 120 pounds, Mary was described by *TV Guide* as "a strapping brunette" when she first appeared on the air. Her measurements were thirty-six–twenty-four–thirty-six —in other words, perfect. She used a special bandeau bra to strap her breasts down and squeeze her bust measurement to thirty inches, and hoped that the costume and her antics would camouflage her obvious femininity.

The sponsors must have been pleased, because they liked the first spot she filmed so much that she did nearly forty more in less than a week, skipping around in ice-cube trays and the like. For this, her first professional engagement, she earned somewhere between six and ten thousand dollars—not at all a bad sum, in 1955. But all too soon there was trouble in Pixieland.

Birth control had been one of the issues over which Mary disagreed with the Church. "I wanted to be free to use it," she says. "So, naturally, I immediately became pregnant." So much for independence. Ironically, Mary's mother formally converted to Catholicism at about this time—and promptly became pregnant also. Mary's sister, Elizabeth Ann, was born just three months before her own child.

As for Mary, she discovered that Hotpoint didn't want a pregnant pixie. "I tried holding my stomach in and everything," she says, "but eventually it was just too obvious. The worst part was that my tummy was starting to pop right out of my skintight leotard.

I looked ridiculous and they let me go." Some other stagestruck hopeful stepped into Mary's pixie shoes and she found herself, just a few months away from the relatively uncomplicated high-school world, married, pregnant, out of work, and on her own in a brand-new life. And parts of it were definitely disagreeable.

She worked hard at marriage, as she had worked hard at dancing. But she hated housework and never felt comfortable in the kitchen. "I know housewives will hate me for saying so," says the woman who became famous as Laura Petrie, America's best-loved housewife, "but their existence is strictly one of sheer drudgery. I'd go out of my mind if that was all I had to look forward to."

Fortunately for her sanity, domesticity wasn't the only thing Mary's future would hold, although she didn't know it at the time. She went on trying to mold herself into the accepted pattern of a good little homemaker in the June Cleaver style, but never really succeeded. And after Richard Carlton Meeker, Jr. was born on July 3, 1956, Mary went back to her dance training and her rounds of auditions, working harder than ever. As Happy Hotpoint, she'd had a taste of show-biz success, and she was determined to make it. As far as further family was concerned, little Richie was a solo performer; it's safe to assume that Mary took advantage of her new freedom from the Church to use birth control.

In 1957, television's heavy hitters were westerns, crime dramas, and variety shows: *The Eddie Fisher Show*, *The George Gobel Show*, and the like. Mary lent her leggy good looks to the chorus lines of these and similar shows for almost a year, before getting her first speaking part—she played Burns's love interest in an episode of *The George Burns Show*. At about the same time, she landed minor parts on episodes of *The Bob Cummings Show* and *Bachelor Father*. But she was still, essentially, a chorus-line hoofer.

Hollywood didn't have roles for as many star dancers, or even dancing actresses, in 1957 as it had in the glory days of the big movie musicals. Broadway might beckon to the ultra-talented few, but Broadway was as yet too distant a dream for Mary. If she were to have a future in show business, she'd have to build it in Los Angeles, where the trend was toward straight acting for television and movies. Regretfully, she says, "I looked around me and I saw dancers such as Shirley MacLaine, Barrie Chase, and Juliet Prowse, and I said to myself that if there's one thing Hollywood doesn't need, it's more dancers." She decided not to buck the trend and switched her goal from dancing to acting. Just like that.

Mary admits that she never studied acting, except as a part of her dance training and her experience with small shows. "I never went the Actors Studio route," she once said. "I'm not an actress who can create a character. I play *me*. I was scared if I tampered with it, I might ruin it. I've always identified with the Thirties—Ruby, Ginger, Fred, Mitzi, all those people. To me, a Brooklyn girl," she added wistfully, "show business meant singing and dancing. The sun rose and set on that Golden Girl dancing her way to stardom."

But, having very sensibly decided to go where the opportunities were, she saw no reason to start over again at square one and begin a lengthy process of acting classes and small-time productions to build up a portfolio. Confident that she could carry out any acting assignment she could get, she did what multitudes of eager job-seekers have done before and since: she faked a résumé.

"It wasn't very hard," she confesses. "I would just mention some obscure play that I'd done in Milwaukee or Chicago. It worked like a charm." In one sense, Mary was already acting—successfully, too, as no one ever called her bluff—and she hadn't even landed her first acting job yet. She offers no apologies for the means she took to get her foot in the door, perhaps because she knows full well that résumé padding (or out-and-out lying) is standard practice in the world of actors, and also perhaps because she feels that the end justified the means. She *did* pull it off, after all. She never let her employers down, and she achieved the goal she set out to reach when she started making the rounds of casting calls with those phony credits. The credits may have been phony, but her talent was real.

Shortly after the appearance on *The George Burns Show*, Mary learned that producer David Heilweil was looking for an actress for a new series he was putting together for Dick Powell's Four Star Films. She was told only that he wanted someone with good-looking legs, nice hands, and a sexy voice. When she arrived on the set for the first time in February of 1959, she discovered why these three qualifications were the *only* qualifications: the role was for a switchboard girl whose face would never be seen by the audience. They would hear her voice but see only her hands and legs. "Well, sometimes they used a little shot of the back of my neck, too," Mary recollects.

The part was Sam, faithful message taker for *Richard Diamond, Private Detective*, played on CBS by David Janssen. Despite the fact that her distinctive, high-pitched, bell-like voice is anything but throaty, Mary landed the part. She tried to sound like Lauren Bacall, but it was her long, lean dancer's legs that clinched the deal.

Sam was conceived of as a gimmick. She would be the one character who would know how to reach Diamond at all times during his exciting escapades—his life would literally be in her hands. But she would remain a mystery to the viewer. According to Heilweil, the gimmick would "whet the viewer's appetite." Mary and her agent were sworn to secrecy. No one was to know who was playing the part of Sam. As part of the secrecy ploy, Mary's name wouldn't even appear in the show's credits.

Even a novice actress with trumped-up credentials didn't have much trouble handling the role of Sam. Mary never interacted with other players on the set. She didn't get to know David Janssen; they never worked together. Mary sometimes did her scenes with her hair in curlers, reading from her script. But the gimmick was working. "Sam" received almost as much fan mail as Janssen did. In fact, Mary insists, even the show's star didn't know her name. He asked her, but her only reply was, "You're the detective, you figure it out." But he finally read it in the newspapers, just like everybody else.

Because Sam made headlines. Thirteen weeks into the first season of the show, she left the cast while

Richard Diamond was still in production, and Roxanne Brooks was assigned to her seat at the switchboard. There are several versions of the story of her departure.

Mary says the reason was money. She was earning the minimal amount of eighty dollars for each episode filmed, or eighty dollars a week. "I was promised more money after the first thirteen episodes," she told the press, "but after we filmed thirteen episodes the producer was replaced and I didn't get the money. So I left."

The studio has a somewhat different version. According to Dick Powell, Mary was courting public attention a little too openly. "She got too much publicity and spoiled the gimmick," he said. Mary countered his accusation with one of her own: "*Variety* printed my name four weeks before the show went on the air, but it didn't 'spoil the gimmick.' "

Whatever the reason, Mary Tyler Moore received more publicity after she left the show than she could possibly have won if she had played Sam for ten seasons. Suddenly, she was a scoop. The trade papers interviewed her, vying to print pictures of "Sam's" face. Two weeks after her final appearance as Sam on May 17, *TV Guide* ran an article called "*Sam* Models the Latest in Hosiery," featuring Mary's legs in colored stockings and frilly skirts. Television's "peekaboo telephone operator," the magazine coyly reported, had already been replaced. Another feature of all this publicity was that it cemented her triple name—Mary Tyler Moore—into readers' memories. Mary had started out at the studio as plain Mary Moore, but soon realized that the name was too bland and unmemorable. She decided to use her full name to distinguish herself from the crop of other acting Moores, notably Terry.

The flurry of publicity over Sam's real identity helped Mary land appearances on other series, mostly dramatic shows. She crowed over earning five hundred dollars for three days' work on an episode of ABC's new series, *Bourbon Street Beat*. She played on other shows, some of which became classics, some of which have been deservedly forgotten: *Hawaiian Eye* (three times), *Surfside Six*, *The Millionaire*, *Wanted: Dead or Alive*, *The Deputy*, *The Aquanauts*, *Johnny Staccato*, *Bronco*, and more. And, with a nice touch of irony, she did appear one more time as Sam. While in the Warner Brothers casting office on other business, she overheard a call from the producers of *77 Sunset Strip* to contact Four Star for the girl who played Sam on *Richard Diamond*. They wanted Sam— not just the actress, but the character too—for an episode called "The Kookie Caper."

Although most of her roles as a guest star were dramatic ones, Mary found herself perpetually playing "good-girl" parts. With that sunny, wholesome face, plumper then than it would be during her hit years, she just wouldn't have been believable as a villainess or a fallen woman. Typical of her work at this time was "The Fix," a *77 Sunset Strip* episode that aired in April 1960.

Mary plays Laura Chandler, an heiress engaged to a surly boxer. She wears tight sweaters, gloves, and lots of jewelry (to show how rich she is). Two of the male characters pantingly describe her as "the end" (to show how sexy she is). But she comes across as simply nice. The show features a complicated plot, but Mary's scenes are simple and emotional. She believes that her fiancé is innocent of murder, even though the evidence against him looks solid, and she pleads touchingly with detective Jeff Spencer to save the big palooka's life.

Mary's biggest scene occurs midway through the show. Laura Chandler is seated at a desk in her plush mansion. Stealthily, a man approaches behind her. He grabs her, gags her, forces her head back (giving the director a nice opportunity to emphasize her cleavage), and points a gun at her head. Then he twists her arm and raises his hand for a blow. The screen discreetly goes black for a commercial, and when the action resumes, Mary has a tiny Band-Aid on her forehead and is holding an ice bag. Ultimately, though, she trades them in for a wedding scene with a corsage and her boxer.

This and a host of similar parts made Mary's face as familiar to TV-watching Americans as her voice and legs already were. Thanks to Sam, she was on her way. "After I left *Richard Diamond*, casting directors started using me because they thought it would be a coup to show the real 'Sam's' face," she said. In all, she landed more than sixty parts in the next several years. Forget Happy Hotpoint—now Mary Tyler Moore was really cooking!

4

MAKE ROOM FOR MARY

Guest appearances, as satisfying as they were, weren't a firm enough foundation for a major career—the kind of career Mary Tyler Moore wanted to have. So she continued to try out for every series part that became available.

In 1959, she auditioned to replace Sherry Jackson as Danny Thomas's daughter, Terry, on his hit show, *The Danny Thomas Show* (formerly *Make Room for Daddy*). The story of how she lost the part by a nose has become a Hollywood legend.

There's something about show business that spawns such legends—those oft-repeated tales of how such-and-such a star was discovered, or how another star turned down a role that later earned an Oscar or a fortune for someone else. Perhaps the public likes to be reminded that there's an element of chance in every success story, hinting that stardom might just possibly come to anybody, at any moment. For whatever reason, show-biz writers and fans have remembered the combination of determination, timing, and good luck that eventually rewarded Mary for missing her first shot at a series part.

Mary auditioned several times in front of Thomas for the part of Terry, nervously joking to her husband that each interview was costing her a can of deodorant. Thomas had doubts about her suitability. As he explained it to Mary, "Nobody could believe that a daughter like mine would have a nose like yours." Mary gamely retorted, "I could have it fixed, to put a bump in it." But Penny Parker got the part.

A year later, in January 1961, the story goes, Thomas was having a haircut in his office at the Desilu studios in Cahuenga. He had a problem. His production company, Calvada Productions, was scheduled to begin shooting in just four days on the pilot for a new comedy series. Every part was cast except one—the female lead! While the barber clipped and combed, producer Carl Reiner, who had created the series, and executive producer Sheldon Leonard entered Thomas's office with a list of the sixty-some young actresses who had tested for the part. Someone asked Thomas, "Can you think of any more?"

The word "more" did the trick. Thomas leaped from his chair and began calling for somebody to get "that girl with the nose and the three names!" The girl was Mary, and the part Thomas was trying to cast was that of Laura Petrie, Dick Van Dyke's wife on the forthcoming *Dick Van Dyke Show.*

Mary was hired almost on the spot at her audition. Recalls Reiner, "She must have thought I was going to kiss her. I looked up, I saw her, I got up, I rushed over, I grabbed her, I said: 'Come on—let's *read*!' "

Mary herself gives some credit to Lady Luck when she says, "I think that as a medium television has a need for certain things at a certain time. The Van

Dyke show needed a girl-next-door type with freck-
les and an average figure, and I was there at the right
time. In other words, luck or something like it is
sometimes paramount, instead of drive or fierce determination." What Mary doesn't say, of course, is
that anyone without her drive and fierce determination would have given up long before she had arrived
at the right place at the right time.

But if Mary believed in luck, Danny Thomas had
a few superstitions of his own. All through the filming of the show's first season, he made a point of
muttering curses, waving his fists, or spitting on the
ground whenever he caught sight of Mary. And he
usually managed to add a penciled insult—"Boo!" or
"Hiss!"—to her weekly paycheck. Why? According
to an old Chinese belief he had come across, the gods
befriend young people who are despised by their
elders. And Thomas wanted to be sure the gods were
on Mary's side.

It was a nice gesture, but Thomas needn't have
bothered. Mary had plenty going for her already, as
he and everyone connected with *The Dick Van Dyke
Show* soon found out.

The show was the semiautobiographical creation of
Carl Reiner, known to audiences from seven years on
Sid Caesar's *Your Show of Shows* and *Caesar's Hour*.
Not only had he acted, he'd done some writing, too,
along with playwright-to-be Neil Simon and Larry
Gelbart, who would later develop *M*A*S*H*. Reiner's idea was to do a show about a television comedy
writer living in a Westchester, New York, suburb—
like Reiner. In fact, the fictional Rob Petrie's street
address was almost identical to Reiner's. And Rob

was named after Reiner's son, who would later act in *All in the Family* and go on to produce and direct comedies of his own.

Mary Tyler Moore, as it happens, wasn't the first Laura Petrie. Reiner sold Peter Lawford on the concept, and Lawford provided the money for shooting a pilot episode in New York—some of that money came from Joseph Kennedy, Lawford's father-in-law. Reiner played Rob, as he had planned to do all along, and Barbara Britton played Laura. Young Gary Morgan played their son. At the office, Rob's zany colleagues were Buddy Sorrell, played by Morty Gunty, and Sally Rogers, played by Sylvia Miles.

The pilot was shown on CBS during the summer of 1960 but didn't make the network's fall schedule. Lawford lost interest, but Reiner held on to the idea, sure that he'd find a new backer. But when Thomas and Leonard came along, Reiner was demoted—or promoted—to the role of Alan Brady, host of the variety show Rob wrote for. The search was on for a new Rob.

The part almost went to Johnny Carson—which might have changed the whole course of television history. But thirty-six-year-old Dick Van Dyke got the part on the strength of his performance in Broadway's *Bye Bye Birdie*, which earned him a Tony award. A gifted singer, dancer, artist, and mime whose hero was Stan Laurel, Van Dyke was also a talented comic actor. In the casting revamp, he was paired with two veteran performers, Rose Marie as Sally and Morey Amsterdam as Buddy. Mel Cooley, Rob's fussy and obtuse boss, was played by Richard Deacon, formerly Lumpy Rutherford's father on *Leave*

It to Beaver. And Larry Mathews was Rob's and Laura's son, Richie, who was just about the same age as Mary's real-life son, Richie Meeker. A publicity article prepared by the studio later claimed that the son's name had been changed to Richie at Mary's request, to keep her from getting him mixed up with her own son and calling him by the wrong name on camera. As the earliest material available on the show's history gives the character's name as Richie, however, it's likely that some not-too-original PR underling simply decided to embellish a coincidence.

Laura, of course, was the last part to be cast. When Mary was chosen, work began frantically on a second pilot.

Up to this point, the show had been called *Head of the Family.* Other names had been kicked around, but none of them seemed to work. Now it was rebaptized *The Dick Van Dyke Show,* in keeping with some of Thomas's other shows—his own, *The Phil Silvers Show, The Joey Bishop Show.* Reiner was the one who insisted on the name change. In hindsight, it seems prophetic, almost as though he knew from the start that Dick Van Dyke was not destined to be the undisputed head of his fictional family. An inexperienced young actress named Mary Tyler Moore was going to surprise everyone by winning just as much attention as the show's ostensible star.

But all that was in the future during the hectic few days of filming the new pilot, which became the show's first episode and aired on October 3, 1961. The New York pilot had shown Rob taking Richie to the office for a day. Another script had been chosen for the Los Angeles pilot, and it happened to feature Laura somewhat more prominently.

Directed by Sheldon Leonard, the show involved a party at Alan Brady's house to which Rob and Laura are invited. Rob feels that they must accept the great man's invitation, but Laura doesn't want to go because she's sure Richie's coming down with a cold. What makes her think so? "He turned down his cupcake," she says worriedly. Of course, Dick is able to overcome Laura's scruples, which seem ever so slightly sanctimonious today, and prevail upon her to come to the party; he is forced to agree to attend two decorator shows and five PTA meetings in return. Clearly, Laura Petrie is not going to be pushed around easily!

Rob, Buddy, and Sally get to showcase their song-and-dance and comedy routines at the party, and Laura gets to pout and look at her watch. But all ends well, naturally, and Laura sweetly apologizes: "Oh, honey, I'm sorry I'm getting to be such a nag." But she adds rather suggestively while removing her pearls and stepping off-screen, "Darling, I'm a woman." The camera fades on Rob's grin.

As comedy, it was pretty standard stuff, except for the hint of sexual magnetism that would continue to simmer through the series, despite Rob's and Laura's decorous twin beds—separated by a table. Also somewhat exceptional in this first episode was the fact that, with few really funny lines and a simple motherhood-and-apple-pie role, Mary Tyler Moore as Laura Petrie was able to hold her own on camera with the seasoned pros. She exuded poise, sincerity, and substance, somehow conveying the idea that Laura

Petrie was not going to be just another anonymous TV wife.

At the time the Los Angeles pilot was filmed, Reiner had prepared a dozen scripts in which Laura fed straight lines to funnyman Rob. But by the time the pilot was being edited, Reiner was working on a script titled "My Blonde-Haired Brunette," in which a bemused Rob reacted with astonishment when his funny wife somehow managed to bleach half her hair platinum in an attempt to make herself more glamorous. Reiner—and others—had immediately recognized Mary's latent comic potential. He began almost from the beginning to modify his original conception of Laura to give Mary more scope. Mary always gave Reiner—and the show's writers and directors—plenty of credit for letting Laura (and Mary Tyler Moore) grow.

The Laura who evolved over the years was amiable, a bit feather-headed, but far less helpless than TV's other female birdbrain, Lucy Ricardo. Laura also emerged as sexy, in a playful, even wholesome way that appealed to men viewers without alienating women. In subsequent scripts she lost manuscripts, innocently blew the cover on Alan Brady's toupee, occasionally indulged her own show-business fantasies, and generally came off as naive but not stupid, affectionate but natural, and most of all, funny.

"It was obvious from the first that we had accidentally stumbled on a kid of twenty-three who could do comedy," Reiner said later. And director John Rich praised her "infallible sense of timing," which he attributed to her background in dance. "She's as sure of herself as an old hand twice her age," he said.

One such "old hand" was Rose Marie, who didn't exactly hit it off with this young dark horse in the show's early days. Marie kept a sign reading "Former Child Star" on her dressing-room door, and insiders on the set soon became aware of an edginess, a suppressed rivalry between the show's two leading ladies. A *TV Guide* writer pointed out that it would be only natural for an older actress to be a little envious of one so much younger, especially when the younger woman was also patently talented. Still, the relationship between the two never flared into outright hostility, and eventually they got along just fine. "Mary's *flowered* as an actress sensationally in the three years of the show," Marie would say, and Mary would politely give public thanks for the opportunity to learn from a pro like Rose Marie.

Some things, though, Mary didn't need much time to learn. "My Blond-Haired Brunette" was the thirteenth episode written and the ninth to be filmed. Yet Mary was so impressive in this show, written especially to demonstrate her comic skills, that it was the *second* episode to be aired. According to Reiner, "If you watch the early *Van Dyke* shows, her development is apparent almost from week to week. She knows where the jokes are."

Morey Amsterdam agreed. "She has more talent in her little finger," he said, "than most girls have in their . . . uh, big finger." And Richard Deacon recalls the initial nervousness that Mary expressed in stiff, somewhat formal behavior: "I watched her start out as a rather—ah—superior little girl, protecting herself against the rest of us, who were all so much more experienced, thinking of us all as hostile, so that she would say, 'Good morning, Deac,' and I wouldn't believe it. And then I saw her gradually acquire confidence and begin to come out and be more open, not only as an actress but as a person. I think of her as a high-spirited filly—but not a difficult one."

From the very beginning, Mary established a working style which she has followed ever since. It has occasionally led to criticism and accusations of temperament, but others have seen it as evidence of her thoroughness and her serious approach to her craft. Jerry Paris, who both directed a number of *Dick Van Dyke* episodes and played the part of Rob and Laura's next-door neighbor, explained: "She's a *thinking* comedienne. Perhaps Laura doesn't think as much as Mary. Mary insists that every line be done in a justifiable way. If something she has to say as Laura doesn't feel right to her, we sit down and reevaluate the line, even the whole scene . . . right up to showtime. She has to do the lines as her own body and mind would react. She's a very tough cookie about this. This doesn't make her difficult—it only makes her a better actress."

As Mary herself has admitted, she's better at playing herself than at creating a character from scratch. It's possible to view this as a limitation, something that keeps her from being able to handle a wide variety of roles. On the other hand, it means that when she finds a role that's *right* for her unique "body and mind," as Paris puts it, she's capable of excellence, as she proved with Laura Petrie.

Despite the unexpected strength that Mary brought to *The Dick Van Dyke Show*, the series started low in the ratings in the fall of 1961 and stayed there all season. In midseason, the network shifted it from Tuesday nights, where it was pitted against the hits *Laramie* and *Bachelor Father*, to Wednesday nights. Procter & Gamble and General Foods, the initial sponsors, weren't thrilled. In March of 1962, CBS's fall schedule appeared—and *The Dick Van Dyke Show* wasn't on it, on *any* night.

"For a few days there, we were canceled," Van Dyke later reported. "We had all almost given up. There was a lot of disappointment for reasons above the loss of income and steady jobs. The chemistry between the people involved—Rose Marie, Mary Tyler Moore, Morey Amsterdam, and myself—was great. We all liked each other."

It's easy to imagine how Mary must have felt at this point. Just a few months after her first really big break, after she'd felt the thrill of working on a new series with established stars, discovering new abilities and potential in herself virtually every day, and earning a lot more than eighty dollars a week—now it was all snatched away, and no amount of drive or hard work on her part could change that. Mary would be the first to admit that cancellations and setbacks are part of the territory in show business—and she herself was to suffer much greater failures and humiliations in the years to come. But at the time, the loss of this first real acting part must have been unbearably painful.

But producer Leonard pleaded with CBS network officials in New York to give the show a second chance, and a new sponsor was found to replace General Foods, which had backed off. The network gave the okay for a second season and kept the show on the air in reruns during the summer. Not long into the second season, *The Dick Van Dyke Show* justified Leonard's faith in it by shooting up in the Nielsen numbers game, finishing the season, incredibly, in ninth place. And at the end of the third season, it was the nation's third-most-watched TV series, surpassed only by *Gunsmoke* and *The Beverly Hillbillies*. Dick Van Dyke and Mary Tyler Moore were America's idea of the perfect couple.

There was an element of unpredictable zaniness in their domestic life, as there had been in the life of the unforgettable Ricardos on *I Love Lucy*. But Rob and Laura Petrie were fundamentally much more ordinary people—they were people that the folks out there in Audienceland could identify with as well as laugh at. True, their situation was pretty mundane by sitcom standards. They weren't oil-rich hillbillies poking fun at the pretensions of the more well bred; they weren't part of a gaggle of soldiers capering around Europe and the Pacific while perpetually trying to put one over on their whining officer. Nor did they offer the standard domestic situation.

For one thing, Richie was very definitely a minor character in the series, as well as an only child—this was one family in which the parents had lives of their own. And Rob and Laura Petrie were younger and sharper—hipper, even—than Donna Reed and Carl Betz of *The Donna Reed Show* or Ozzie and Harriet Nelson.

By today's standards, *The Dick Van Dyke* show seems oppresisvely cute, and feminists would surely take issue with Laura's eternal wifeliness, which is summed up by an episode called "My Part-time Wife." In it, Sally goes on a leave of absence to appear as a guest on the late-night "Stevie Parsons Show," and Laura persuades Rob to let her take Sally's place in the office—temporarily, of course. Her ability to keep everything running smoothly at home while performing wonders at the office upsets Rob, until she confesses that she slaved over the cooking and cleaning late at night in secret and only took the job "to help my husband." Not exactly Mary Richards talking, but at the same time Laura manages to come off as a real person, not a Lucy Ricardo caricature.

It may have typified the suburban, middle-class setting and old-fashioned values that Norman Lear would blow apart with *All in the Family* and others of the next generation of sitcoms, but *The Dick Van Dyke Show* incorporated wit, style (in fact, fashion as represented on the show was an important part of its appeal), and a modicum of sophistication. Coming up with high-quality scripts, avoiding hokey or repetitive story lines, wasn't always easy.

Carl Reiner wrote something like forty scripts for the first two years of the show on his own—after all, *The Dick Van Dyke Show* was, in some ways, the "Carl Reiner, This Is Your Life" show. He then began to use the writing team of Sam Denoff and Bill Persky (Persky is now writing for, among other shows, *Kate and Allie*). Like Reiner, Denoff and Persky drew heavily on personal experience for story ideas.

"You can't have an experience without trying to relate it to the show," Persky said at the time. "I had a flat tire on a deserted Mexican highway not long ago. All the time, I was scared to death, but I kept thinking, 'How can I put this in the show?' " Even the director's experiences helped. Howard Morris directed a segment called "Scratch My Car and Die," about Rob's new roadster. "I got a new Thunderbird that week, so I knew how it felt," Morris said, and added, "You go through a tiny psychoanalysis when you start one of these things. You have to base comedy on reality. In drama, you can get away with things—Tennessee Williams can write about cannibalism or weird sickness, but we know that to get people to laugh, we must help them identify with the situation."

And according to Denoff, the key to identification was feeling. "The only good shows are the ones that deal with the high emotions," he said. "We keep a notebook full of premises—story ideas—like this one: 'Rob and nude of Laura.' That became a strong script about Rob running the gamut of emotions when he hears that there is a nude painting of his wife in a local art gallery. The idea clicked right away."

"But how many ways can you write a jealousy show?" Persky asked. "Or an embarrassment show? Or a love show? Sometimes we all go for days without coming up with a good idea."

Persky and Denoff had put their writers' fingers on the dilemma of the sitcom: without a dramatic premise, such as crime or danger, it's easy for a series to get bogged down in look-alike plots. Sitcoms have a built-in life expectancy. If they outlive it, they start to become stale. Both Dick Van Dyke and Mary Tyler Moore would be wise enough to recognize and accept that truth at crucial points in their careers.

Yet while their show soared in the ratings, both

the star and Mary, his second banana, were content
to bask in the glory of good reviews and critical
acclaim.

They earned enough press clippings to fill a shelf
of scrapbooks apiece, but they also earned more,
individually and together: recognition from their peers
in the entertainment industry and the prestige that
came with it.

In 1963 and for three successive years, *The Dick
Van Dyke Show* was voted the outstanding comedy
series by the Television Academy. Mary and Van
Dyke were nominated for Emmy Awards in 1963.
Both lost. Shirley Booth, the poker-faced housemaid
of *Hazel*, beat Mary out for best leading actress. But
in 1964 Mary was nominated again, and won over
Booth, Irene Ryan, Inger Stevens, and Patty Duke.
That same year, she received the Golden Globe Award
as best female television star. She won a second
Emmy in 1966. Van Dyke also won an Emmy in
1966. Indeed, the annual Emmy ceremonies became
something like family reunions, with Mary, Van Dyke,
Reiner, and the rest of the cast and company congrat-
ulating and thanking each other. Mary didn't have a
college diploma to hang on her wall, but in less time
than it would have taken to graduate, she had won
enough awards in her field to decorate a fair-sized
mantelpiece.

The Dick Van Dyke Show spawned masses of news
paper and magazine articles, most of them stressing
the One-Big-Happy-Family angle. There was a lot of
truth in it. If Mary needed to run an errand with her
son, the shooting schedule could be rearranged to

accommodate it. Van Dyke himself was a family man, with four children, and they frequently visited the set, as did Richie Meeker. Mary mostly passed her spare time on the set with Ann Morgan Guilbert, who played the Petries' neighbor, press-ganging cast and crew members into playing games like Perquacky. All good, clean fun.

In fact, in all of the publicity surrounding the five-year run of the show, only twice was Mary described in less than sugary terms. One incident took place during a short-lived attempt to kick her heavy cigarette habit. She hadn't had a cigarette for five days, and she was delivering her lines badly during a scene with Dick. "I was just *saying* the lines, phoning them in," she admits. Reiner asked what was on her mind and she shouted at him, "I can't be responsible for the lines!" A fairly trivial little outburst, all things considered. Yet once home, where she immediately lit up a cigarette, Mary called Reiner to apologize.

Her other temper tantrum occurred over a script that called for Laura to get her toe stuck in a bathtub. Although she had many funny lines, they were all delivered from off-camera, and Mary made it plain that she didn't want to do any more scripts that put her out of sight.

As far as her costars were concerned, Mary remained a private, closed-off person, an expert in the fine art of being polite yet aloof. She spent a lot of time in her dressing room, never sought out or shared personal problems, and only invited the cast to her home once. Yet she was universally liked and respected. She just wasn't *known*. One barrier to intimacy was her earnestness about the big career she was certain she was going to have. She wasn't egotistical, she was simply determined and confident. Her nickname among cast and crew members was "Mary Tyler Moviestar."

Much of the show's early publicity focused on Mary's shapely legs and well-rounded derriere—and the tight Capri pants she showed them off in on the show. Mary had long favored casual wear. In fact, just two weeks before the *Dick Van Dyke* pilot aired, she was featured in a puff-piece in *TV Guide* called "Pants, Pants, Pants." It showed Mary, described as "a long-stemmed dancer-turned-actress who wears pants well," modeling several sets of slacks that were nowhere near as snug-fitting as the ones that would arouse the "Capri controversy" once the show was under way.

As a chorus-line dancer, Mary had been accustomed to show up for rehearsals in casual pants that showed off her legs. She came to rehearsals for the Van Dyke show the same way, and at some point someone decided to let her wear the short, tight slacks on camera. But it so happened that at that time sponsors made a practice of surveying the families of employees about shows in which their commercials appeared. Procter & Gamble learned from one such survey that some Procter & Gamble wives were offended by Mary's Capris.

"Well, for a while I put away the Capris," Mary recalls. "Then Carl got a flood of letters—oh, I'd say anyway seventeen letters"—a perfect Laura Petrie joke—"from fans who wanted to know why I wasn't wearing them." The pants were reinstated, possibly causing some renewed panting among Mary's male viewers, and fashion magazines reported that stores all over the country began doing a brisk business in "the Laura Petrie look."

For all its innovations and successes, *The Dick Van Dyke Show* eventually came to a close. Its star decided to leave his series while it was at its zenith and pursue a movie career. Although the decision to quit while he was ahead may have been a wise one for Dick Van Dyke, his movie career never really took off. In fact, his personal and professional lives were to go sharply downhill. Oddly enough, Mary was the only one of the Van Dyke cast who would go steadily on to bigger and better things.

She didn't know that at the time, though, and despite the fact that she had often said, "I don't want to play Laura Petrie for the rest of my life," she was saddened when the show ended. She'd done more than 150 episodes in the life of Laura Petrie; she'd worked side by side for five years, often late into the night, with her colleagues; she'd learned and grown and prospered.

"Saying how I feel about the Van Dyke show is like saying how I feel about my family," she was to say one day years later—except that she looks back more fondly on the show than on her family life. "It was my childhood in the business, my growing-up time, the happiest period in my life." And despite the slight but perceptible distance she had always maintained between herself and the others on the show, she wept with them when the final episode was filmed.

"It was like breaking up my family," she said. Sadly, Mary knew what breaking up a family meant. Her own family had broken up just months into the show's first season.

5

A Change of Partners— and Parts

Mary has refused to say much about why and how her first marriage ended. Richard Meeker she describes only as "a nice man, a decent man," and, like her siblings, he is a somewhat vague and shadowy figure in her own accounts of her life.

Mary has always credited him with being a good father to their son and with staying involved in Richie's life. "Richie lives with Dick now when he wants to," she reported not long after the breakup, and Richie was to spend a great deal of time with his father during his teen years.

Mary's marriage to Dick Meeker had three strikes against it from the start.

First, Mary was only seventeen when they were married. As any statistician will easily demonstrate, marriages in which one partner is that young don't generally last very long. As Mary herself puts it, "Dick had already done a lot of his growing. I'd done none, and we grew in different directions." In a favorite metaphor, which she also uses to describe her differences with both her son and her second husband, she adds, "We simply read different books, Dick and I."

Second, Mary had married hastily and, as she puts it, "to get out of the house." Dick Meeker might have known what he wanted from life, but Mary didn't give herself time to get to know him or to understand why she had agreed to marry him. Her career hadn't taken off, her life at home was intolerable, so she rushed into marriage hoping for security but unprepared for the reality of married life and motherhood.

Third, life is never easy for the nonfamous mate of a famous person. And when the marriage takes place in the pressure-cooker environment of Hollywood, where one partner's life is full of the glamorous trappings of show business and the other's is a nine-to-five stint in an everyday office, the problem is intensified. Mary has denied that the split was due to her own growing success, and it's true that she had by no means arrived at superstar status when the separation took place. But she had appeared in plenty of television shows and been touted in dozens of articles as a rising star. Perhaps Meeker saw the writing on the wall and didn't relish life as a Hollywood husband.

There were certain fundamental differences between Mary and Dick Meeker that simply didn't go away. One of the largest concerned guns and hunting. Mary has always been devoted to the cause of animal protection; in fact, she once stated that one of the three things she liked best about herself was her refusal to wear furs, which she called "symbols of vanity and cruelty." (The other two things were her willingness to work hard to achieve a goal and her public appearances on behalf of hospitals and charities.) But Dick Meeker was an enthusiastic sport hunter who collected guns, and Mary found this passion of his not only incomprehensible but indefensible. It's ironic—and tragic—that Meeker passed his interest in guns along to their son.

Mary determinedly tried to overlook this and other problems between herself and her husband, just as she feverishly redecorated the house they had bought, trying to turn it from Spanish-style stucco into French Regency. Although she wanted to cover things up, she was as unable to change her house as she was to remain married.

Whatever the reasons, Mary and Dick parted. Regardless of her Catholic upbringing, she sued him for divorce in February 1962. Did a new romantic interest spur Mary toward the divorce?

Mary has always claimed that she met Grant Tinker after separating from her husband. The fact is that they kept their relationship very quiet at first. She says that's because they both feared people would leap to the conclusion that Mary had left her husband for Grant and he had left his wife and four children for her. Whatever the truth of the matter, before Mary's divorce from husband number one was final, she had fallen in love with husband number two.

Mary hadn't even liked Grant Tinker when she first met him.

He was an executive with Benton & Bowles, an ad agency that handled one of the advertisers on the Van Dyke show. He was a suave, well-bred easterner, at home in the world of show business and an astute businessman. He and Mary met on the set of the series. "I knew he was somebody I was *supposed* to be nice to," she says, "and I think that's why I disliked him so much. Also," she adds, revealing her own characteristic insecurity about her lack of higher education, "I hated him for being so educated and for wearing such perfect neckties."

Shortly after, while Mary was in New York doing publicity for the show, Grant asked her for a date. She was surprised, but said to herself, "He thinks he's so hot, I'll show him."

What Mary planned to do was something rather childish and manipulative, something that Laura Petrie would probably not have approved of. She decided to have one fabulous date with this well-educated, perfect-necktied man—and then drop him. "I was going to really wow him on that first date," she recalls. "I'd be so great that he'd ask me for a second one. Then I'd turn him down. But it didn't work out that way."

In fact, Grant took her to Broadway to see Barbara Bel Geddes in *Mary, Mary*, and she took him to the Peppermint Lounge, where they didn't exactly twist the night away. Mary's plan not only didn't come off, it backfired entirely. "I woke up the next morning and knew I was in love," she says.

Mary and Grant were married quietly in a civil ceremony at the Dunes Hotel in Las Vegas on June 1, 1962.

What turned Mary's thinking about Grant around? She's made no secret of the fact that she was powerfully attracted to his virile good looks—"he's still great looking," she said a little wistfully years later, after their divorce. And no one could deny the powerful bond of affection and mutual admiration that infused their marriage. But like Dick Meeker, Grant was more than ten years older than Mary. And he was more powerful, more polished, and more sophisticated than Meeker had been.

In marrying a second older man, this time one who was also successful and authoritative, Mary was repeating—even amplifying—the pattern she had set in her first marriage. She was creating a relationship to substitute for the "close, loving relationship" that she didn't have with her father. It's significant that among the things she initially hated about Grant were his eastern background and his education—qualities she has always associated with her father. In effect, Mary was marrying Daddy.

It's easy to understand the attraction of such a mate to a woman like Mary. Not only did his love make up for the love she feels she didn't receive from her father, his superior age and experience made him the perfect protector. Mary has always had a tendency to leave matters of personal business such as bill paying, investing, and so on in the hands of her male advisers, men like Grant and her longtime business manager, Arthur Price. And an older man might be especially appealing to someone who has admitted that she thinks of herself as "average looking" and "not very feminine," and therefore perhaps not very comfortable with boys and men her own age.

It's noteworthy, too, that Dick Van Dyke was thirteen years older than Mary—a fact that may have contributed to their on-screen chemistry. Her character, Mary Richards, was more involved with the much older Lou Grant than she ever was with any of her many swains. And Mary's closest working relationships have always been with the men—usually older—who were not her costars but her producers and directors, men who controlled or guided her in various ways.

Whatever the factors that drew Mary and Grant together, they were married just months after her separation from Meeker. Grant took up a new job as West Coast programming head for NBC, and the couple moved with Richie into a small house with a swimming pool in the Hollywood Hills, the first of many, many homes they would share. What with the Van Dyke show renewed for the next season, a new husband, and a new home, Mary was on top of the world in the summer of sixty-two.

Her home life over the next few years was incorporated into the *Dick Van Dyke* publicity machine.

While she played America's premiere housewife on-screen, Mary got a lot of mileage out of the fact that at home she was anything but a typical hausfrau. "I hate to cook," she said often, citing melted cheese sandwiches and an entree called "Poor Man's Beef Stroganoff" as the only things she could prepare in an emergency. "I'm perfectly happy to have someone come in while I'm chatting with my husband and tell me a perfect dinner is served," she reported, adding, "afterwards, someone else can do the dishes."

Only once, she recalls, did she actually have to cook on the show—most of the time her kitchen activities were strictly pretense. But on one occasion the script called for her to prepare some scrambled eggs for Dick. "They weren't what you'd call a rousing success," she admits. "We planned a five-minute scene, working at the stove and getting it to the table. But we acted much faster than we should have and the eggs were nowhere near being ready when I had to dish them out on a plate. It was quite a problem—what I really needed was a soup bowl! But Dick ate them, bless him, and only turned a little green."

Grant usually contributed his bit to interviews of his wife by saying something like, "Mary and Laura have a lot in common, actually, except Mary doesn't serve me my breakfast with merry quips."

Perhaps in an attempt to distance herself from the very domestic Laura, Mary made no bones about the fact that "I'd rather sit down over a cocktail at the end of the day than struggle in the kitchen," and she didn't attempt to hide her heavy smoking habit—still regarded as somewhat unladylike in the early 1960s.

As far as entertaining was concerned, Mary suffered a kind of party anxiety that Mary Richards would later express perfectly. On the one occasion when she did invite her coworkers over for a party, Mary ordered everything out from a Mexican restaurant. She chatted with her guests in the living room until it was time for dinner, blithely assuming that they'd find everything ready in the dining room. But to her dismay, all they found was cartons of food, left sitting on the kitchen floor by the delivery men. Mary was hard put even to locate enough plates and forks for her guests. "We didn't let her forget that in a hurry!" Van Dyke later laughed. "I'll say he didn't," Mary grumbled. "He wrote 'Needs Soap' in the dust on top of my refrigerator."

Mary bought Grant a banjo and the two were photographed with it—he strumming, she smiling,

Richie in the background. Mary told reporters over and over again, "My husband and I have nothing we really *do* for fun. We talk a lot." She insisted that she enjoyed just spending time with Grant, and the two shunned the never-ending round of Hollywood parties.

"Grant's my best friend," she would say. "I really enjoy his company and his mind." And she revealed a certain paternal quality in his treatment of her when she said, "When I come home in a really bitchy mood and announce, 'Do you know what happened today, what so-and-so did to me?' he'll say, 'It beats not workin', kid, have a martini.' "

During the *Dick Van Dyke* years, the Tinkers moved into a large house in Encino. Mary exulted over the "fifty-six feet of closet space" in her room and explained that they needed a big place to allow for visits from Grant's children. At the same time, she found their affluence somewhat disturbing.

In fact, shortly after moving into the new house she said, "As a Brooklyn-born person who never had much, it worries me that my child—maybe children— will grow up in such an atmosphere. I half wish we could live on a normal street. My husband and I talk about it—but nothing ever comes of it. It's insular, this community, even though it is a great place to raise kids. But it's not preparing them for life. Beverly Hills is a fantasy town: big cars, big houses, possessions, pampering—no preparation for life. Those of us who have motivation did not necessarily come from wealthy backgrounds." Her misgivings ironically foreshadow the difficulties that were to come between her and her son, Richie, in just a few more years.

Mary confesses to having felt a tremendous amount of insecurity about her place on *The Dick Van Dyke Show*, in spite of all her successes. She even turned down guest appearances on other shows if they required her to be written out of a series episode. "I don't want to give up even one Van Dyke show because I'm afraid the audience might learn to like it that way," she said at the time.

But she was equally leery of being permanently typecast as Laura Petrie, so she did put in guest appearances—when they didn't conflict with her shooting schedule. She even received an offer from Broadway producer David Merrick to star in a new musical—but she turned him down because she expected to be busy with the series.

What she really wanted, though, was to make it someday in the big-time world of show business: the movies. After all, wasn't she Mary Tyler Moviestar? So when, in 1964, CBS announced that the 1965–66 season would be the last for *The Dick Van Dyke Show*, Mary was thrilled to be signed by Universal Studios for a ten-picture, seven-year contract—at a guaranteed $100,000 per picture. She, for one, wouldn't be at a loose end when the series was over. Like Dick Van Dyke himself, she was moving on to the big screen. She hoped to do light comedy—"the type of thing that Myrna Loy and William Powell used to do."

The contract was reported in all the grade papers and gossip columnist Hedda Hopper made a prediction that must have made Mary very happy—she predicted that MTM would be TNT in movies. "I want to be the next Doris Day!" Mary is said to have announced, and David Merrick claimed that she would be "the next Mary Martin." What no one seems to have been sure of is what Mary Tyler Moore would be like as herself.

"I want to be a big star," Mary said enthusiastically, "so I can surround myself with interesting, exciting people and properties from a business standpoint. If neglecting television in the future would ensure my success in movies, then I would never appear on television again. However," she added, somewhat prophetically, "I have no fears about doing another television series. I know I could always do one if that's the way things work out. As far as movies are concerned, we'll have to wait and see. I could knock myself out in front of the cameras, but unfortunately it's the box-office receipts that are going to make the difference."

Mary had already had some knowledge of movie cameras and box offices. In 1961, she had appeared in *X-15*, a highly forgettable movie, in semidocumentary style, about the lives and loves of staff members at a California missile base. The lead part went to a high-altitude rocket.

"It must have been the worst picture in film history," Mary says with a grimace. She's not a professional critic, but the show's miserable performance at the box office confirms her opinion. "If it's ever shown on television," she advises, "make sure you go out that night."

Now, in 1966, she was ready for her second film— her first under the new contract. It sounded perfect: a musical comedy produced by Ross Hunter, directed by George Roy Hill, with music by Sammy

Cahn and Jimmy Van Heusen, starring musical greats Julie Andrews, Bea Lillie, and Carol Channing. It was even set in the Roaring Twenties. To Mary, who had cherished fantasies of being one of "those Golden Girls dancing into the sunset," *Thoroughly Modern Millie* was irresistible.

During the filming, Mary became friendly with Julie Andrews, unmistakably the star of the picture. But Mary got a little taste of star treatment, too, and reveled in it. "A studio car picked me up every morning," she reminisced a few months later. "My dressing room was as big as our living room at home and, on the first day of shooting, all the studio executives sent flowers."

Audiences responded fairly well when *Thoroughly Modern Millie* was released in 1967. It was a troubled year in America, and while some moviegoers flocked to shudder at Warren Beatty and Faye Dunaway as playful psychopaths in *Bonnie and Clyde* or to watch Anne Bancroft seduce a nervous Dustin Hoffman in *The Graduate*, plenty of others seemed grateful for a silly, old-fashioned musical, and *Millie* did well at the box office.

It was something less than TNT for Mary, though—more like a handful of cherry bombs. Her performance received moderately favorable reviews, but she generated no excitement. She was cast as the wimpy, whispery, aristocratic roommate of a gutsy flapper, played with some vigor by Julie Andrews, who dominated the film's singing and dancing. The ridiculous plot involved an attempt to kidnap Dorothy, Mary's character, by a white slaver played by Bea Lillie. The question the film never answered, however, is

why any self-respecting white slaver would bother
with the feeble Dorothy in the first place—it's clear
that she'd be far more trouble than she was worth to
any harem. She's rescued by Millie, played by thoroughly modern Julie, and matched up at the end
with John Gavin.

The role was clearly secondary, and weak to boot.
Yet Mary brought nothing to it but an ineffectual,
sugary niceness. It's as though she tried very carefully to suppress all of her "Laura Petrie" manner-
isms in taking on a new role, but didn't have anything
to put in their place. So, while George Roy Hill
went on to direct *Butch Cassidy and the Sundance Kid*
and Carol Channing was nominated for an Oscar for
her supporting-actress role in *Millie* and Julie Andrews calmly chalked up another success, nobody
was wild about Mary. In fact, her business manager
Arthur Price later claimed that the movie "did her
great harm," saying, "All that sweetness and light
scared people."

But although Mary was to go on playing vapid,
good-girl characters in her next several movies, she
took time out first to cross the country to tackle a
completely different role in a whole new medium.

Grant was transferred back to New York to a job
in the network's corporate headquarters in Rockefel-
ler Center. So Mary called David Merrick to ask if
the role on Broadway he had offered was still available. She auditioned—"a horrible rendition of 'Blue
Skies,' " she remembers—with a bad bronchial cold
. . . and got the part.

If she had known the magnitude of the disaster
that lay in wait, she might well have stuck to her

needlepoint or hastened back to television. Or maybe not. There has always been a streak of masochism in Mary Tyler Moore, as she herself knows, and perhaps she wouldn't have wanted to spare herself the worst drubbing of her professional career.

6

Holly Go Quickly

Holly Golightly is still something of a Broadway legend.

Producer David Merrick sank more than half a million dollars into a musical adaptation of Truman Capote's novella *Breakfast at Tiffany's*, which had been filmed in 1961 with Audrey Hepburn and George Peppard. In place of the movie's Oscar-winning theme, "Moon River," by Henry Mancini and Johnny Mercer, the musical would feature songs by Bob Merrill, of *Carnival* and *Funny Girl* fame. And *Holly Golightly* was written and directed by hit-maker Abe Burrows, who had *Guys and Dolls* to his credit.

With all this tried and true stage talent at his disposal, Merrick took a bold step when it came to casting his principals. Although he halfheartedly denied that he was trying to lure Broadway-shy television fans into the theater, the strategy was obvious. Instead of drawing on the pool of available stage actors, he would take his stars from the tube and hope for a crossover audience. For the part of Jeff, the young writer who tells the story, Merrick chose Richard Chamberlain, known to millions as *Dr. Kildare*. And for the role of Holly Golightly, the cynical, confused waif who "dates" men for fifty dollars a shot, he wanted Mary Tyler Moore, the all-American girl next door.

The contrast between Mary's well-scrubbed image as Laura Petrie and her newest role as a neurotic nympho brought the show plenty of pre-opening publicity. Amazingly enough, Mary reported to *Newsweek* that she and Holly were "not terribly dissimilar." Holly, Mary explained, wasn't really a tramp or a prostitute. "She just happens to develop friendships with fabulously rich guys who give her five hundred dollars every time she goes to the bathroom instead of a quarter," said Mary, sounding like Laura Petrie at her most naive. Holly was really worth a lot less to her "dates" than $500. "She's a fun girl, a personality girl, and I can play that."

Chamberlain was a bit more realistic in his assessment of Holly. "Mary's doing such a wonderful job," he reported during rehearsals, which took place at the Mark Hellinger Theater on Fifty-first Street. "She's playing a hooker, you know. Let's face it, a hooker." Chamberlain, too, was coping with the demands of singing and of working in a new medium and under intense scrutiny. Critics and show-biz observers were saying of both the new show's stars: will they make it? And, as always, there were many watching and waiting to pounce on failure.

Mary's eagerness to succeed—and possibly also her never-abandoned dream of becoming a dancer—caused her to work obsessively hard in preparation for the show's opening. In bleak, crowded backstage conditions, a far cry from the luxury she had experienced in Hollywood, she went through her paces again and again and again. She shrieked her lines, straining her throat to achieve the projection demanded of stage performers. "She lived that play day and night," Grant Tinker says. "She worked till midnight, and when she came home she worked some more."

Mary had other worries besides the show. In a very short period of time, she'd had to pack up the family's Encino house, get them settled into the twelve-room Fifth Avenue apartment they sublet from former NBC president Robert Kintner, and enroll Richie in a private school. Even the Tinkers' German shepherd and miniature poodle had to attend obedience school to learn how to walk on leashes after having had the freedom of a huge yard in California. "I guess I should have gone to school to get Manhattanized, too," Mary remarked.

She was uncomfortable living in New York, shying away from the aggressive autograph hunters, shuddering at the raving street people, shivering at tales of violence, East Coast style. "A man who works with my husband got mugged at 125th Street the other night," she told an interviewer. "He was just trying to catch a train home, that's all. Lord, I hope I don't end up with an ice pick in my heart!"

Her homesickness for California (and perhaps a growing uneasiness about the show, as well) emerged in a classic example of the "Freudian slip" one day during rehearsal. Trying for a line that read, "I'm going back to *Brazil*!", Mary shrieked, "I'm going back to *California*—I mean, Brazil!"

As hard as she worked at becoming Holly, Mary showed a certain squeamishness, even prudishness, at certain aspects of her role. In a scene where Holly is led offstage by a policewoman, Mary was supposed to yell, "Take your paws off me, meter maid. Quit shoving me, you dirty tramp!" One day she stopped rehearsal to ask if "meter maid" and "tramp" could be dropped. "I mean," she explained, "we don't want to suggest that all meter maids, in this country are tramps. I know I sound moralistic, but that's how I feel."

Not surprisingly, the stage manager was less willing to accommodate Mary's "feelings" about her lines than the *Dick Van Dyke* staff had been. The lines stayed in.

During this time, while Mary put in long rehearsal days every day and Grant settled into his new job, it was Grant who spent evenings with little Richie. He recalls the two of them sitting in the quiet apartment and staring at each other across the table, wondering how Mary was doing. The separation from her family was greater than it had been when she was playing on television; that, on top of the sudden relocation to New York, can only have added further strain to her nerves.

Mary also recounted a series of disturbing dreams that occurred during the play's preparation and that might have offered fertile ground for speculation if she had been inclined to self-analysis in those days. In one of them, she said, "I dreamed that poor old Morey Amsterdam from the Van Dyke show was going down the kitchen drain. Literally. Finally, all I could see of him was a huge eye disappearing down the sink. . . ." Maybe the dream meant only that Mary was lonely for the safe, comfortable days on the Van Dyke show. Or maybe it meant that she had a premonition that very soon, something would be going "down the drain"—and it wouldn't be Morey Amsterdam.

The show was to open in Philadelphia and have a short run there and in Boston before the official Broadway opening. Traditionally, these out-of-town openings are supposed to give everyone a chance to iron out the wrinkles in a new show; in Mary's case, the wrinkles kept getting worse.

After rehearsals began in Philadelphia, where the show was to open, Mary had another dream: "I dreamed I was in an airplane crash on an island. Then suddenly all these bears got inside and rafts came out of the ceiling. I got on a raft and made it safely back to the mainland." If the "crash" reflects Mary's fear of failing in the show, her escape on the raft points to her strong instinct of survival, which was to stand her in good stead. She also mentioned a recurring nightmare from which she'd suffered periodically "practically all my life," as she puts it. It seems to offer a tantalizing glimpse of what makes Mary Tyler Moore really tick.

"I'm on a beach," she describes it, "and these huge tidal waves come in. I fight, but they carry me away. I claw at the sand, and yet they take me away. I don't know why I dream it. I love the sea." Analysts say that the sea often figures as a symbol of life, of fate—the forces beyond our control that shape our lives. It's characteristic of controlled, disciplined Mary that, like the legendary King Canute, she would attempt to fight the sea, and with as little success. But perhaps the very fact that she is on the beach in the first place, and that she loves the sea, suggests that underneath her veneer of control there's a part of her that longs to be swept away in spite of herself. The desire to control and the desire to be overpowered are the basic drives of Mary's personality.

While Mary dreamed by night, rehearsals went on by day. Mary had been plagued by growing nervousness, and Chamberlain had a bad cold. When, in Philadelphia, Mary developed her own severe case of laryngitis, she tried to soothe it with everything from throat sprays to honey to Julie Andrews' own favorite lozenges. Julie, herself a veteran of many long-running theatrical productions, had sent Mary a silver box from Tiffany's filled with the lozenges as a good-luck gift. Poor Mary, though, would need more than a lucky lozenge to cope with what lay ahead.

Meanwhile, things looked great at the box office. Publicity and word of mouth had done wonders, ringing in sellout advance ticket sales. Despite the illness of both leads and the general shakiness of the production, which no amount of rehearsal had been able to iron out, the stage seemed to be set for a smashing success on opening night.

The first performance was a disaster. Chamberlain and Mary came onstage to generous applause, but the show went downhill from there. Suddenly it became apparent that Burrows' broadly comic script was unsuited to Capote's sardonic, sophisticated story. And choreographer Michael Kidd's dance numbers clashed with everything. To make it worse, Mary could hardly sing. At one point, a member of the audience loudly suggested voice lessons. In short, as a stage debut, it could hardly have been worse.

Still, Mary showed her stuff by bravely completing the performance, forcing herself through each song despite the pain in her throat, never missing a line or a cue. She even managed to summon up a watery smile at her curtain call, which she took to

minimal applause. At last it was over. "Well, we got
it up there," Burrows announced backstage. "Now
we got to work." Capote, who had watched the performance, didn't seem too upset. "I predict the show
will run fourteen months," he said. "A successful,
but not distinguished, musical." Asked whether Mary
fit his idea of Holly, the author replied: "Oh, everyone has known a Holly Golightly. One has passed
through everyone's life. Now this girl may not be
your Holly or mine—but she's possibly someone's."
He added that Audrey Hepburn hadn't been his idea
of Holly, either.

The Philadelphia critics savaged the production,
and Mary, and Holly. Mary managed to finish the
short Philadelphia run, but worse was to happen in
Boston. Meanwhile, Merrick decided that *Holly
Golightly* needed a name change. The show became
Breakfast at Tiffany's. But the Boston critics were able
to recognize what they called "a straightforward musical flop" no matter what its name, and they panned
it mercilessly. At this point, Merrick felt that more
than just the show's title needed surgery. What if
needed, in fact, was a whole new script.

Edward Albee, author of *Who's Afraid of Virginia
Woolf*, was called in to rework the libretto—an odd
choice on Merrick's part, as Albee had never written
a musical. Still, perhaps Merrick thought he could
come up with something like Capote's own dark version of the story. And while Burrows stayed on for a
short time as director, he eventually left, to be replaced by Joseph Anthony. Burrows later claimed
that his version (written with his partner, Nunnally
Johnson) had commercial potential, although he con-

ceded that it had received "somewhat mixed" reviews. Albee's version didn't have that problem—the
reviews were unanimous.

While still performing the original Burrows–Johnson
script in Boston nightly, the cast daily rehearsed the
new Albee script—distinguished chiefly by the "frank-
ness" of its dialogue, which was to shock audiences
and startle even blasé reviewers. The demands of this
high-pressure sort of work, especially in the face of
hostile critics and audiences and mounting anxiety,
would have taken their toll on even the most hard-
ened stage veteran. They devastated Mary, who
claimed that the month in Boston had seemed longer
than a year. "I'll be afraid to go into Sardi's," she said
just before returning to New York. "Everyone will
be looking at me and saying, 'Poor girl.' " She added,
"I've got to clear my name. It's been the roughest
period of my life."

It got rougher.

The new, "improved" version of the show played
for the first time in New York to preview audiences.
Mary was unprepared for their hostility, which was
expressed in everything from Bronx cheers to shouted
barbs to laughter at the play's most dramatic moments. A more experienced actress might, just might,
have been able to separate her sense of self-worth
from the shambles of the production and get through
it with some degree of fortitude. But it crushed Mary.

"I don't think anybody ever played to the kind of
rudeness we put up with," she says. "It was humiliating." She told a reporter that the out-of-place laughter was the hardest to deal with: "It's the most crushing
blow an actor has to endure—I don't think I could
face it again."

She didn't have to face it for long. So much of the audience walked out during the second preview performance that Merrick, describing the show as "an excruciatingly boring evening . . . my Bay of Pigs," announced that the third preview would be the final performance. The show was closed before it had even opened.

For that closing night, an audience described by one Broadway figure as "ghouls" descended on the theater to witness what *Newsweek* called "the show-business equivalent of the sinking of the *Titanic*." Only there were no lifeboats when *Breakfast at Tiffany's* went down. There were just two ovations during the entire evening. One occurred when a bed refused to move and the stagehands almost had to kick it to get it to budge. The audience clapped derisively when it finally slid free. The other ovation took place when the cast applauded Mary at the last curtain.

Trouper that she is, Mary showed up for the cast party—more like a wake—at Sardi's. She even managed to keep smiling. "I'm feeling all the things you can imagine I must be feeling," she told a reporter, with some asperity. "All I can say now is that I want to be with my friends and share in some warm good-byes." Everyone involved in the fiasco rode it out with dignity; there was an absence of the finger-pointing and recrimination that one might have expected to follow such a flop. Merrick joked that Cartier's had begged him not to close the show—because they were sure it would ruin their rival's reputation. Mary and Richard Chamberlain said over and over that they didn't blame Merrick, Burrows, or Albee for the show's problems or its demise. All agreed that it was nobody's fault that the play just hadn't worked out.

There were massive losses, of course. Once the advance ticket sales had been refunded, the show's backers (principally Merrick) were in the red to the tune of $400,000. An RCA Victor record contract also went down the drain. And while Hepburn had enhanced her reputation and earned an Oscar nomination as Holly in the movie, both Mary's and Chamberlain's reputations were hurt because of the show.

The two stars also took an emotional beating. The tension of attempting something new and trying to live up to the world's expectations, followed by the strain of months of difficult rehearsal, and culminating in the show's disastrous reception and its early closing, left both of them battered. Chamberlain told Rex Reed, "I got very manic and uptight. I walked past the marquee to see my name in lights for one last time, and then I cried all night." Of course, Chamberlain was to have many well-deserved successes later in his career, but the debacle of *Breakfast at Tiffany's* cost him several years of psychoanalysis.

Mary paid a high price, too. She shouldered the burden of the failure. As she told a reporter a few months later, "I've felt that maybe it was my fault that my show didn't survive." That must have been a crushing burden for a success-oriented perfectionist to live with. But Mary resolutely went on with her life. She turned herself into an East Coast–style matron, clipping her distinctive shoulder flip into a severely short cut and trading in her slacks for dresses and pumps. She spent time with Richie and bought him ice skates for the pond in Central Park, right across the street. She tried to enjoy New York.

"The shopping is great and it will be good to see shows while they're new," she said. "Richie and I are going to take horseback-riding lessons. I must get a book that describes the dishes on French menus. I've met a couple of potential friends, people I've liked and would like to know better. Dick Chamberlain and I are going to take Richie to Radio City Music Hall. I've already started ballet classes—you know, the real kind where if you don't sweat and hurt all over, you're not doing it right."

This flurry of activity is typical of Mary's need to keep herself busy. "I hate to loaf," she says. During the Van Dyke years, her longest breaks were the three-month vacations between seasons. "The first two weeks I'd let out all Richie's clothes and shop for something that would never be used," she recalls. "After that, I'd be dying to get back to work." Riding lessons and Radio City weren't enough to keep Mary happy.

In early 1967, she made her second movie for Universal, an eminently forgettable farce called *What's So Bad About Feeling Good?* Filmed in New York, it starred Mary and George Peppard—badly miscast somewhere between beatniks and hippies—and a magic toucan that scatters happiness instead of birdseed all around it. In the meantime, *Thoroughly Modern Millie* was almost ready for release and Mary was now at a loose end.

"As for Broadway," she said firmly, "I'd do another show tomorrow if I could." But it was to be a long time before Mary gave her regards to Broadway again.

7

Homecomings and Heartbreaks

Perhaps the best gift Mary could have received during that grim Christmas season in 1966—other than a successful run of her show on Broadway—was a plane ticket back to the West Coast. Despite all her attempts to enjoy it, she had never really taken to life in New York. Brooklyn-born or not, she thought of herself as a California girl through and through. So she was thrilled when Grant told her soon after the first of the year that he was leaving NBC to accept a vice-presidency at her own studio, Universal—and that they would be moving back to California, just months after relocating to New York. "Does this mean I won't have to wait for the elevator every time I want to walk the dogs?" Mary asked him.

They were back in Hollywood by March, renting the house that Dinah Shore and George Montgomery had lived in and replacing their urban pallor with their standard mahogany-colored tans. Mary's lifestyle flip-flopped again—she put away her dresses and pumps and retrieved her slacks and sandals, and she let her hair grow.

Mary's third film, *Don't Just Stand There!*, was released in May 1968. It was another saccharine, characterless role, as though the producers at Universal had decided that watered-down Laura Petrie (with a shot of Doris Day thrown in for good measure) was Mary's destiny. Unfortunately, in wisely trying *not* just to recreate Laura every time she stepped in front of a camera, Mary came off as bland, cute, and sickeningly sweet. In *Don't Just Stand There!* she rescues a female pornographer from smugglers in a plot similar in some ways to that of *Millie* but even less plausible, if that's possible. Mary does wind up in a clinch with the male lead—baby-faced Robert Wagner—but that didn't make up for the fact that she couldn't hold her own on-screen against Glynis Johns as the sex novelist.

Mary showed no eagerness to return to television. She was convinced that her future lay where the *real* stardom was—in movies. But during 1967 and 1968, Mary was forced to reassess her plans. *Millie* opened, and didn't make Mary a star overnight. *What's So Bad About Feeling Good?* and *Don't Just Stand There!* played during the summer of 1968. Both did poorly in the reviews and at the box office—which was only natural, as they were pitted against major-league stars and great comedies. *Funny Girl*, with Barbra Streisand, and Mel Brooks's instant classic *The Producers* also opened that summer. On the heels of her disastrous venture on Broadway, the lackluster reception her movies received led Mary to examine her life and her career. Richie was twelve years old, she and Grant had been married for six years . . . Mary decided it was time to have another child.

Mary has never revealed her deepest feelings about

having children, or discussed her reasons for deciding to have a child. It may have been that she truly wanted another child; she had spent relatively little time with Richie during his early childhood.

As soon as he was born, she began dancing and working on television, with a schedule that kept getting busier and busier. When he was in elementary school, she'd been on the set of *The Dick Van Dyke Show* for most of every day during three-quarters of the year, snatching a few hours with her family in the evenings or occasionally on weekends. Did she regret having missed so much of the time she could have spent with the baby and the little boy who had grown up along with her career? Perhaps she longed for another child in part so that she could experience more of the day-to-day joys of motherhood, sharing her baby's childhood more fully. It may even be that the problems that were shortly to disrupt her relationship with Richie had already begun to surface and Mary wanted to start over again with a new child.

Another possibility is that she wanted to cement her marriage to Grant with a baby of their own. She had Richie, and Grant had children from his first marriage. Did Mary feel a need to share the bond of parenthood, perhaps the most basic of human connections, with this older man, this father figure whose approval was so important to her? Or was the rift between them, which would lead to separation a few years later, already beginning to open? If so, perhaps Mary felt that a child would help her to close it again.

Whatever her motives, Mary quickly became pregnant. She and Grant were ecstatic. But their happiness was short-lived. Mary's pregnancy ended fairly early in a miscarriage. She was rushed to the hospital in an ambulance and suffered the loss of her baby—the baby that she and Grant had made so many wonderful plans for.

If her nightmare on Broadway had been Mary's most crushing professional defeat to date, then here was a personal loss even more devastating. Aside from the sheer physical pain and the fear she must have felt, it's easy to believe that Mary—always the perfectionist, always her own most severe critic—saw the miscarriage as another tragic failure. She had failed as an actress, and now she had failed as a woman, too.

Still worse was to come. In the grip of the depression and grief she naturally felt at losing her baby, Mary learned that she was ill—seriously ill. Routine blood tests administered after her arrival at the hospital showed that she was a diabetic. She had suffered from a serious case of juvenile diabetes—the kind where the pancreas doesn't work at all, and the blood sugar balance is constantly disturbed—for some time without being aware of it. In fact, the disease probably caused the miscarriage.

"Apparently, I'd *always* had diabetes," Mary says, "though I never felt sick, just sometimes a little weak and tired." She was shocked when the doctors told her she had the disease. For one thing, she didn't understand what diabetes meant or how diabetics lived. She envisioned her future as an invalid and the prospect horrified her.

"My doctor put me on a drug called Orinase, which is taken orally," she recalls. "I was put on a strict food regimen that forbade me to have sweets, which I adore, or a drink, which I always enjoyed after a day's work. I couldn't deal with it." Mary, who had always imposed self-discipline on herself, was now being told that her whole life had to change because of something inside her that she couldn't control at all, her disease. She reacted in a characteristically self-destructive way.

"I spent the next couple of months sneaking cookies, then sitting in the parking lot and eating them," she says. "I can't believe I was so stupid, but I literally ate myself into a state of collapse. And then I was *really* sick." Mary's doctor put her on insulin treatment and told her that she'd have to give herself two shots of insulin every day for the rest of her life. She refused to learn how to use the needle and insisted on coming to the doctor's office twice every day for her shots. Eventually, however, the inconvenience of this arrangement wore down her resistance and she trained herself to administer the shots. She has done so ever since. But, although she began seeing a psychiatrist in order to come to terms with her medical condition, she wasn't able to control other aspects of her destructive behavior.

Eating forbidden foods and drinking alcohol remained problems for Mary until recently. Not only did she develop hard-to-break eating and drinking habits over a period of many years, but she also used food as a weapon against herself and others, the way many anorexic and bulimic women do. As she recognizes, her problem is tied up with the issue of control and self-discipline. "I don't know why I binge, but in a funny way—this is just a guess—bingeing is part of

control," she speculated in 1980. "I sort of step outside myself and say, 'Nobody's going to tell *me* what
I want to eat and I am therefore going to have six
doughnuts *right now*.' Maybe it's part of thumbing
my nose at doctors and at fate. I want so much
control that I don't have to be controlled if I don't
want to be." And a few months later she publicly
rationalized the act of sharing a hot fudge sundae
with Andy Warhol by saying casually, "I'll just take
a little extra insulin tonight."

Because she herself was so uncomfortable with her
condition, Mary deeply resented the field day that
the movie magazines and tabloids had with it: "Some
of the fan magazines made it such a big deal," she
says. "It became a circus of stories about Mary Tyler
Moore's disease and hints about how I was at the end
of the line." But over time Mary did learn that diabetes is not the specter she had feared, that it can be
controlled, that diabetics can lead normal lives. "You
have to pretty much map out your exercise, your
diet, and your insulin intake, and balance those three,"
she explains. "But if you can do that, you're going to
be a healthier person than most nondiabetics, and
there's no reason why you can't do anything you
want with no limits."

Mary has come a long way from her initial refusal
to accept the reality of her disease. Since 1984, she
has been a spokesperson for the Juvenile Diabetes
Foundation, donating her time and services for many
television, magazine, and fund-raising appearances.
"There *is* a cure, and we'll find it," she assures viewers in her TV spots. And there is no doubt that the
support of a much-loved star like Mary not only

helps the organization but also helps other diabetics deal with their illness.

Mary never became pregnant again. It has been suggested that damage caused by the miscarriage may have left her unable to have children. But barely a year later, when asked by a reporter if she planned to have more children, Mary coolly replied, "At my age, thirty, I can't afford to take a year out of my career." Some years later she confessed, "Grant and I wanted a child very much. We tried, for several years. But apparently, because of my diabetes, I just wasn't capable of having children anymore. Oh, it didn't crush either of us. It was just . . . a disappointment." But this disappointment may have made the eventual loss of her only child, Richie, harder to bear years later.

She also now wishes she had been able to have a daughter. "I'd have liked that very much—to be a mother of someone of my own sex," she says wistfully. "I'm attracted to men because of their 'otherness' —and I raised an *other*, a male child. I'd like to have seen the instinctive female parts of a person develop from infancy."

No mention was ever made of adoption in the Tinker household, though. Instead, Mary put her broken dreams of maternity behind her and decided to move ahead in her career.

Her next venture was a movie with Elvis Presley. Called *Change of Habit*, it was released in 1969. It still shows up fairly frequently on television, usually early in the morning or on Sunday afternoons, and even this limited exposure is due not to Mary but to the fact that it's one of the "Elvis movies," if possibly the worst.

Elvis was cast against type as a sideburned, singing surgeon who works with poor people in a Puerto Rican *barrio*, apparently because his late army buddy had been a poor person from a bad neighborhood. There are only three songs in the movie—all terrible. Ironically enough, in view of her strong anti-Catholic feelings, Mary plays Sister Michelle, a nun who is determined to "reach" today's troubled society by doing good deeds without telling people she's a nun. With two sister sidekicks, played by Barbara McNair and Jane Elliot, she ventures into the ghetto to work at Presley's clinic.

The best part of the movie is probably the opening credits, which run over a stripteaselike scene. As Elvis croons the title song, a nun is shown from the shoulders down (shades of "Sam"!) changing from her old-fashioned habit into secular, though dowdy, garb. The final shot shows Mary removing her tight nun's headgear and shaking out her familiar, neatly parted flip. The movie goes downhill from there. Predictably enough, Elvis and Mary fall in love, but all chemistry is lacking in their few romantic scenes. Mary remembers Elvis as a "sweet, lovable bear of a man," but very polite—"If you weren't careful, he'd start calling you 'ma'am.' " Mary's dilemma—to choose the Church or Elvis—doesn't seem particularly important, and in fact the movie ends before she decides. Interestingly, this was the first of Mary's many appearances with Ed Asner, who played the amiable local cop, Lieutenant Moretti.

Predictably, the movie was not very well received.

It didn't offer enough of Elvis to excite his fans, and no teenage girl could identify with Mary as a prim nun. One critic called it *"The Sound of Music* goes slumming."* Elvis moved on to other things, and so did Mary. She appeared on television in *Love, American Style* in 1969, and she filmed a mediocre suspense thriller for TV called *Run a Crooked Mile* with Louis Jourdan. It was shot in London and shown in 1970. It must have seemed to Mary at this point that nothing had gone right for her since *The Dick Van Dyke Show* ended.

Ironically the next big leap in her career came through Dick Van Dyke. CBS planned to reunite her with Van Dyke—for a special to be shown in April of 1969. Called "Dick Van Dyke and the Other Woman," it featured singing, dancing, and comedy and was produced by Sam Denoff and Bill Persky, who had written so many episodes of *The Dick Van Dyke Show*. Eight years after they had first worked together, MTM and DVD were back together again.

While Mary had been making mediocre movies and coping with personal and professional crises, Dick Van Dyke had also tried to promote his movie career. It had gotten off to a great start with *Mary Poppins*, filmed between two seasons of the series, but then it seemed to stall. He was also having family problems. Although the world didn't know it yet, he was suffering from alcoholism. But when he approached CBS executives with the idea for a "reunion" special, they smelled success; after all, *The Dick Van Dyke Show* was still running in syndicated reruns on daytime TV all over the country. And they were right. Viewers loved Dick and Mary dancing, clowning, and recollecting the good old New Rochelle days as Rob and Laura. The special scored phenomenally well in the ratings and suddenly everyone remembered that Mary Tyler Moore *did* have some successes on her track record.

The reunion with Van Dyke may have given producers a clue that television comedy was Mary's strong suit. At any rate, all three networks called her to offer her the pinnacle of TV success—her own series. Suddenly, just three years after leaving the small screen for a humiliating rejection on Broadway and a string of disappointing movies, Mary was hot again. And this time she was in a position to call the shots—or to have Grant Tinker call them for her.

NEW YORKERS, JEWS, MOUSTACHES, AND DIVORCED PEOPLE

Mary had been seeing a psychoanalyst since her miscarriage. Her therapy had helped her cope with the realization that she was diabetic, but it hadn't done much toward resolving her larger uncertainties about her life and career. "I went to him because I was scared," she explained. "I thought, if I'm not going to be an actress, what or whom am I? I wasn't a hostess, a gardener, a cook or a full-time mother. I had my needlepoint and my crossword puzzles—hardly what you'd call a career. Luckily the TV show came along and I didn't have to worry about it."

Just after her triumphant television special with Dick Van Dyke, the phone rang off the hook with offers from CBS, ABC, and NBC. Mary decided that work was the only therapy she needed and gave up her analysis, which she described as "scenes from some theater-of-the-absurd play." It was time to concentrate on a brand-new series. Along with her analysis, Mary shelved the remainder of her Universal movie contract.

With Grant's help, she reviewed the network's offers and accepted CBS's, a multimillion-dollar deal which guaranteed her not only ownership rights to the new series but also creative control. By retaining the ownership rights, Mary had the chance to make a huge fortune if the show was successful and went into syndicated reruns—that's how TV mega-stars like Lucille Ball and Jackie Gleason made their fortunes. Mary signed on the dotted line in September 1969.

Grant, now a vice-president at Twentieth Century–Fox, Mary, and Mary's business manager, Arthur Price, formed a new production company to develop the show and named it MTM Enterprises in honor of Mary. Grant recruited two writers from Fox to work on the show: Jim Brooks and Allen Burns, who had collaborated on *Room 222*. Each had dropped out of college to go to work as a page in a network office—Burns at NBC, Brooks at CBS. And each had held other jobs that they drew on for inspiration during the early days at MTM.

Brooks had worked as a reporter-writer in the CBS newsroom, about which he says, "It was like being a kid in a toy store. There was no caste system, no bureaucracy, in the newsroom. Everybody shared their feelings with everybody else." He was able to recreate some of this cheerful anarchy in the fictional WJM newsroom. Burns got comic training working as a writer-artist for Jay Ward, owner of Rocky and Bullwinkle, Dudley Do-Right, and "Fractured Fairy Tales." "Anything went at Jay Ward's," he recalls. "There were no taboos. The more bizarre, the better. That was a great period in my life—it freed me totally." Burns would help make "no taboos" a battle cry at MTM over the years.

Amazingly, CBS had committed itself to a full season of Mary's show—without a single script, or even a story idea. The only things definite about the show at that point were that Mary would be about thirty and that she'd be living in Minneapolis—a real community, unlike the fictional Mayberrys and Mayfields of so many sitcoms, yet an off-the-beaten-track one, less of a cliché to viewers than the typical East Coast–West Coast big cities of other series. And Mary herself issued the only other qualification—"I didn't want to do another husband-and-wife show because I was afraid it would be unfavorably compared with the *Dick Van Dyke* series."

Now the first order of business for Burns and Brooks was to come up with the show's premise. And they hadn't even met Mary yet. "The trust she had in Grant—to put these two total strangers in charge of launching her career," Burns marvels. "A good thing she wasn't in on some of our first sessions. Boy, did we come up with some useless ideas! Like, Mary was going to be an assistant to a gossip columnist. Or she was going to play the field, dating two guys simultaneously—which one would get her?" Mary ruled out children, roommates, a fiancé.

"Then we latched on to divorce and we knew we had a winner," Burns says. "Every writer in town had a divorce story on the drawing board. But we had the actress it would work with!" In early 1970, Burns and Brooks took their exciting new idea to the CBS executives in New York—a group of people who had never been noted for their innovativeness or daring.

"Well, we sat there in a room full of divorced New York Jews with mustaches," Burns remembers, "and heard them say that there are four things Americans don't like: New Yorkers, divorced people, men with mustaches, and Jews. It was strongly hinted that if we insisted on having Mary divorced, the show would go on at one in the morning." Burns and Brooks weren't big enough yet to fight the network on this one and win.

Burns continues: "At that point Jim and I really wanted to quit the show. I mean, Mary couldn't be married, since she was still coupled with Dick Van Dyke in the eyes of the public, and people might think she had divorced him, and *nobody* divorces Dick Van Dyke. And we insisted on having her over thirty so we could make her a real adult. And it was already the year of the widow—remember Doris Day and *Julia*? We just didn't want to have to kill another man off to get Mary on the air.

"Finally, it occurred to our male-chauvinist minds that a girl could be thirty, unmarried, and have a past involving men. Then we hit on the idea of the newsroom, and we liked it immediately because it wasn't one of those TV jobs where the people never work." So WJM-TV was created and Mary's show was under way.

Although the MTM team tried to come up with a clever title for the show, none of their ideas seemed suitable, so—remembering what had worked for Dick Van Dyke and a host of others—they billed it as *The Mary Tyler Moore Show*. But in June 1970, a few months before the start of its first season, the show was renamed just *Mary Tyler Moore*. The former full title, Mary explained, was too grandiose. "It sounds as if it should be accompanied by a blare of trumpets and a long drumroll," she said. "It gives the impression of a great big deal. It's larger than life, and I'm not." While the name change was chalked up to modesty and just-folksiness, it also resulted in a title that was somehow more sophisticated and contemporary, that helped to set the show apart from its predecessors. It's probable that Mary knew this perfectly well.

By this time, Burns and Brooks had developed a past for the character Mary Richards. In the first episode, she was to move to Minneapolis, into an apartment in the building where an old girlfriend lived. The girlfriend—and landlady—was Phyllis, played by Cloris Leachman. Mary would be trying to put her life back together after the next best thing to a divorce, the breakup of a long-term love affair. The dialogue makes it clear that Mary had helped put her boyfriend through medical school for several years, the implication being that they lived together, but that when she indicated that she was ready for marriage, his response was: "Let's not rush into anything." So she dumped him and struck out, hopefully but with some trepidation, on her own.

Her job search lands her in the newsroom of station WJM-TV, where she fails to land a job as a stenographer. But irascible station manager Lou Grant, played by Ed Asner, offers her the job of associate news producer—for fifteen dollars less a week. The other newsroom characters are briefly introduced.

Later Mary meets her upstairs neighbor, Rhoda. As a foil for Mary (and perhaps as a tongue-in-cheek defiance of those network executives) Brooks and Burns made this character, played by Valerie Harper, a New Yorker who was also very obviously Jewish. She was also a bit dumpy, very mouthy, and very funny.

Much about that first episode was to change as the show developed over the years. Mary would trade in the early miniskirts and go-go boots as styles changed. Eventually she would even move from her "bachelorette" studio into a more stylish high-rise apartment. Lou would metamorphose from a hard-drinking boor into a gruff but lovable father figure. When Valerie Harper returned from a vacation tan, slim, and beautiful, Rhoda's transformation into a stylish beauty began. Other characters similarly gained depth or were allowed to change and grow.

But much of the enduring tone for the seven-year run of the series was set in a few perfect moments of the first show: when Lou asks Mary, in his office, if she'd like a drink to celebrate her new job, she diffidently asks for a Brandy Alexander—he just looks at her and pours a shot from the bottle in his desk. Just before Mary's ex-boyfriend, Bill, arrives on a visit, she coolly unbuttons the top button of her blouse—then nervously buttons it up again before he shows up. Lou and Mary's relationship was sealed forever when he said, "You know what you've got, Mary? Spunk." And while she blushed prettily and murmured, "Oh, thank you, Mr. Grant," he added, "I hate spunk."

Moments like those would keep happening in every episode of *Mary Tyler Moore*, and would help make it one of the most popular sitcoms ever. And one brief scene from the first show lingered until the very end in the opening credits. No matter how her hairstyle and clothing changed with the years, Mary never cut out the shot of herself standing on a street corner and jubilantly tossing her knit cap into the air.

One of the strengths of the show was a quality it had in common with *The Dick Van Dyke Show*—a strong set of ensemble players who received roughly equal shares of time and attention. Something less than half the action took place in Mary's apartment, where she coped with dates (usually washouts), parties (usually disasters), Phyllis (whose brother was gay and whose adulterous Swedish husband provided not only plot material but also opportunities for Leachman to do a hilarious mock accent), and Rhoda (usually putting herself down, but amusingly). The rest of the show revolved around the newsroom and the brilliantly bizarre crew who populated it.

"We went around to newsrooms all over Los Angeles and researched the characters," says Burns. "In every one we found a Ted, a Lou, and a Murray." Ted, played by Ted Knight, was the buffoonish newscaster, the butt of everyone else's jokes but too obtuse to realize it; Murray, played by Gavin MacLeod, was the quiet, sardonic writer, a little bitter about his low place on the literary totem pole. "There were Murrays in all the newsrooms," Burns recalls, "muttering under their breath when the anchorperson

sailed through the studio, wafting cologne after him."
As for Lou, the tough guy with the soft heart, Burns
reports that "even Walter Cronkite told us that his
managing editor was just like Lou."

Preseason publicity about the show wasn't universally encouraging. Many people speculated that it
would be too sophisticated for a middle-American
audience, that great majority of viewers who were far
from silent about what they liked and didn't like on
TV. One TV observer, Herb Jacobs, predicted that
Mary Tyler Moore would be the first show of the
season to be cancelled. And the first preview before a
live audience confirmed these portents of doom. Not
only did the audience not like the show much, Mary
herself wasn't crazy about it—particularly the character of Rhoda, whom she found brash and unsympathetic (there has also been speculation that Mary
might have feared that Valerie Harper, playing a new
kind of character, would be so funny she'd steal the
show). She insisted on a rewrite, so Burns and Brooks
emphasized the mutual dislike of Mary and Rhoda at
their first meeting—Rhoda was furious because Mary
had rented the apartment *she* wanted. As Harper and
Mary worked together over the years, both their
off-camera and on-camera friendships flourished and
added a very real element of warmth to the show.

The show was slotted for Saturday night, opposite
NBC's *Saturday Night Movie* and ABC's *The Most
Deadly Game*, with George Maharis. In reality, Mary's
fears of another *Holly* were unfounded. The premiere
was well received and the show climbed steadily in
the ratings throughout the season. And, buoyed by

their success, Brooks and Burns went to the mat against the network censor to defend their controversial story lines.

"In all fairness," Brooks reported later, "most of our trouble was with one guy, not the whole network brass. He tried to kill two of our shows in that first year. One was 'Support Your Local Mother,' in which Nancy Walker played Valerie Harper's mother. The guy said, 'This is the most tasteless Jewish-mother routine I've ever seen.' The second show he tried to kill involved Mary going out with a short guy, maybe five feet two inches tall, and our friend at CBS said, 'You can't have Mary dating a deformed person.' Apparently, he had read only the title of the segments, 'Toulouse-Lautrec Is One of My Favorite Artists.' To their credit, the network brass overruled our nemesis. And do you want to know something funny? It was those two shows that won the Emmys that year for us and for director Jay Sandrich."

Another show that season involved the first in a long series of dreadful parties at Mary's place. Perhaps drawing on her own lack of domesticity (remember the cartons of tacos and burritos?), Mary brought a touching blend of hope and anxiety to these stories, which were always audience favorites. In the first of them, Rhoda invites a date to Mary's party—and he brings his wife. The magnitude of the disasters Mary faced as a hostess would escalate over the years.

Everyone involved in the development of *MTM* agreed that, to be fresh, the show must avoid perpetuating the stereotypes of earlier sitcoms: the work-free jobs, the never-wrinkling clothes, the noncontroversial subjects. "The only issue I care about," Jim Brooks said, "is that we don't recreate the old Ozzie and Harriet myth of the ideal family in the ideal world." And, pointing to one of the show's greatest strengths, Mary said, "Jim and Allan and I agreed on most important things. None of us would ever write in a gratuitous putdown just because it was funny or satirize something that was pathetic. The characters have a lot of affection for each other and we don't want to destroy that." Mary was talking about integrity—a quality that viewers instinctively respected and responded to in both Mary Richards and her world.

Mary Tyler Moore, one of the year's most-talked-about new shows, finished the season in twenty-second place in the Nielsens and was nominated for Emmy Awards in almost every category. On the night of May 9, 1971, Ed Asner (best supporting actor), Valerie Harper (best supporting actress), director Jay Sandrich (for the short-date episode), and Jim Brooks and Allen Burns (for writing the Jewish-mother episode) carried Emmy statues home. Sadly, *MTM* and Mary had lost to the season's other new supershow, *All in the Family*, and Jean Stapleton. The same scenario would be repeated the next year. Not until 1973 did Mary take home an Emmy for *MTM*. By 1975, the show and its creators and players had won a total of twenty-three Emmys.

Regardless of her chagrin at the Emmy Awards in 1971, however, Mary was riding high after her first season back on television. Her old partner, Dick Van

Dyke, may have been a little jealous—he did joke that he'd love "to sabotage that show and get Mary back." He paired up with Hope Lange during the 1971–72 season on *The New Dick Van Dyke Show*, but the show never got off the ground. While some critics had speculated that Mary's early success was due to Dick, she proved that she could fare better without him than he did without her. He went on to flop badly on Broadway in *The Music Man*.

As for Mary, she continued to charm audiences as Mary Richards. "I'll be acting naturally and instinctively in the role," she had said before the series premiered. She was hoping to attract a loyal following on the strength of her personality, realizing that clever story gimmicks and big-name guest stars can't carry a sitcom forever. When asked whether she felt she had the qualities necessary to appeal to an audience week after week, or whether those qualities had been built into Laura Petrie, she had replied nervously, "I don't want to examine it too closely. If a performer begins to think about those things, it could spoil everything."

Mary's nervousness about her ability to woo viewers proved to be unfounded. Burns and Brooks wisely chose to capitalize on Mary's natural charm—her decency, politeness, and modesty as well as her comedic skills—in tailoring the scripts to her character. They wrote what Burns calls "good attitude lines" for her. "She's funny when she's in a situation where she is vulnerable, tired, angry, surprised—she can play those attitudes with a very funny slant," he said. "And she surprises us. We don't always write those

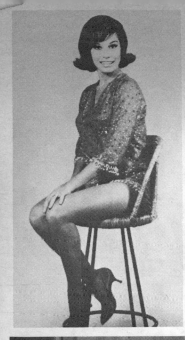

Mary's legs got her career going, but not in the way she imagined. Though dancing was her first love, her long, lovely limbs landed her the role of the Happy Hotpoint lady—a pixie who danced on a stove. Her more famous role, however, was as Sam, **Richard Diamond, Private Eye**'s faithful but mysterious assistant; only her voice was heard and her legs were seen.

As Laura Petrie on **The Dick Van Dyke Show** from 1961-66, Mary Tyler Moore became a household name.

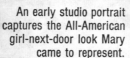

An early studio portrait captures the All-American girl-next-door look Mary came to represent.

One of Mary's dreams came true when she played opposite Julie Andrews in **Thoroughly Modern Millie** in 1967. Although the film did well at the box office, Mary received only minimal recognition next to Andrews, Bea Lillie, and Carol Channing.

Mary Tyler Moore with her only son Richard in 1967. After Mary's divorce from Richard's father, Richard Meeker, her son chose to live a quiet life with him.

Backstage with parents George and Marjorie at **A Taste of Honey** in 1981.

Mary is reunited with longtime co-star Valerie Harper in 1985 at the Golden Apple Awards luncheon

TV audiences were charmed by the girl from the Midwest chumming with a wisecracking Jewish girl from Manhattan . . .

. . . and years later, sparring with a chain-smoking copywriter (Katey Sagal) in Chicago.

America has also seen Mary switch bosses: from a hard-boiled, fast drinking TV news producer (Ed Asner) . . .

. . . to a smooth-talking, romantic newspaper editor (James Farentino).

As Mary's career met success and failure, her personal life also underwent some changes.

She and Grant Tinker enjoyed an often-photographed marriage that ended in 1980 after eighteen years.

All eyes were on Mary and her new beau, cardiologist Dr. Robert Levine, fifteen years her junior, when they were married on Thanksgiving Eve, 1983.

Despite the ups and downs of Mary's personal and professional lives, she has always emerged smiling, the symbol of her optimism and resiliance.

attitudes into the script. Sometimes she just comes up with completely offbeat responses."

Occasional guest stars added some of the sparkle to *MTM*. Among them were Henry Winkler and Penny Marshall, in the period before they made it big in series of their own; Eileen Heckart, who played Mary's aunt and a minor romantic interest for Lou; Johnny Carson, whose voice was heard during a blackout at one of Mary's pitiful parties; even First Lady Betty Ford, who talked to Mary on the phone in one of the show's funniest and most memorable episodes. Nanette Fabray, seventeen years Mary's senior, appeared as her mother in the show's third season. Over the years, she had a few boyfriends, including Ted Bessell (Marlo Thomas's former steady on *That Girl*) who lasted more than one episode. None of them was ever serious, though—Mary Richards remained single. A San Francisco TV anchorman said, "Every newsroom has its Ted Baxter anchorman, a boss like Lou, and a woman like Mary. There is a tacit understanding that we will not date her, but we sure all do hope she will remain single."

Today, looking back on her years as Mary Richards, Mary Tyler Moore says, "We all know I spent a number of years playing a character who wasn't very far removed from myself. Even today, I sometimes find myself thinking, 'Would Mary Richards do that?' She was—is—very real to me." And she was clearly very real to her television viewers. The show worked so consistently well in part because Mary Richards *was* Mary Tyler Moore. She had all the warmth and authenticity of a real person, someone who was funny but vulnerable, beautiful, but not threateningly or one-dimensionally sexy, who faced just-barely-believable situations with an appealing mixture of fallibility and wit—someone who was perfectly summed up in her broad trademark grin.

If Mary Richards was Mary Tyler Moore, however, the opposite wasn't necessarily true. Although the two coexisted peacefully for some time, there was more to the woman behind the smile than appeared in her most famous character.

THE KITTEN THAT ROARED

Like all new companies, MTM Enterprises needed a corporate symbol or logo when it was formed. In a lighthearted parody of "Leo," the roaring Metro-Goldwyn-Mayer lion who appears on the screen at the end of every MGM production, MTM's sign-off featured a tiny, mewing kitten in a ribbon garland. That little kitten was destined to become a lion in its own right in the entertainment industry.

The history of MTM is a capsule history of the best of contemporary American television. Norman Lear may have broken new ground with outrageous subject matter and outspoken scripts in *All in the Family*, *The Jeffersons*, *Maude*, and other sitcoms, but MTM consistently set new standards of production quality and explored innovative programming possibilities. MTM shows became known for their thoughtful humor, which was more often a result of carefully developed characters than of one-liners.

MTM's first venture in addition to Mary's show was the popular and successful *Bob Newhart Show*, which in 1972 began appearing in the time slot after *Mary Tyler Moore*. Newhart played a psychologist in a format rather similar to Mary's—his show dealt partly with his wacky office mates and even wackier patients and partly with his wife, played by Suzanne Pleshette, and his friend, played by Bill Daly. Like Mary, Newhart is an "attitude actor" rather than a stand-up comedian, and like Mary's, his show derived much of its humor from his patient, logical reactions to the craziness of the people around him. Although the show went off the air after five seasons—at Newhart's instigation—he returned to television several years ago with a new wife and a Vermont inn in the sitcom *Newhart*, also an MTM Enterprises production. Newhart has managed to personalize the MTM sign-off, though. Instead of the kitten's mew, the audience hears his own inimitably dry voice saying "Meow."

Valerie Harper's popularity on *MTM* at times rivaled Mary's. It earned her an MTM spinoff series of her own, *Rhoda*, which started high in the ratings in 1974 but later sagged. Unlike Mary, Rhoda turned in her single state for a TV marriage—which didn't work out. In the typcal MTM mode, she was surrounded by a cast of offbeat characters with well-developed comic personalities of their own. (Interestingly, one of the funniest minor characters on *Rhoda* was both an echo of Mary's long-ago "Sam" and an inside joke with her son. "Carlton, your doorman," the stoned concierge, played by the show's coproducer Lorenzo Music, was heard but never seen—and Carlton, of course, was Richie's middle name.) Cloris Leachman, too, was given *Phyllis*, which did less well than *Rhoda*. Harper managed to swing a series deal for her friend, Paul Sand, for whom MTM put together *Paul Sand in Friends and Lovers*. It bombed. Other early MTM failures were *The Texas Wheelers* and an attempt to reprise *Hogan's Heroes*, called *Second Start*, later *The Bob Crane Show*. During the 1970s, MTM tried for another mega-hit with *Doc*, *Three for the Road*, *We've Got Each Other*, *The Tony Randall Show*, *The White Shadow*, *WKRP in Cincinnati*, and *The Betty White Show*. While none of them—except perhaps *WKRP*, still hugely popular in syndication—made television history, such was MTM's status that the studio continued to draw support for new projects, even as some of its ventures failed. It got so you couldn't watch television for long on any night of the week without hearing the squeaky "meow" of the MTM kitten.

The failures, however, were modest; the successes (especially the ongoing success of the studio's flagship, *MTM*) were spectaculor. *Lou Grant* was the first television spinoff to jump genres and take a character from a half-hour sitcom into an hour-long dramatic series. And in 1981 MTM would score a gigantic winner with the much-acclaimed *Hill Street Blues*.

Even before then, MTM had shaped some important aspects of television, perhaps even of popular American culture as a whole. For one thing, *MTM* had broken the unspoken rule that said that all TV shows took place either in Small Town, U.S.A., or in New York or Los Angeles—the latter two being inexpensive choices, as most studios were located in Los Angeles, with a scattering of production companies and the network headquarters located in New

York. Instead, MTM's shows broke the setting barrier and took place in Chicago, Philadelphia, or San Francisco. Even more important, the MTM shows depicted—and by depicting, helped to create—the first yuppies.

Mary Tyler Moore appealed to a new breed of TV viewer—someone who took it for granted that a woman (or a man) could reach thirty without a spouse or family, that living alone could be satisfying, that friends could provide the framework that family had once supplied, that dating was an activity for grown-ups, not just teenagers. And the characters on MTM shows were, for the most part, young, urban professionals who worked hard to surround and clothe themselves with the appurtenances of the sophisticated life. In short, life for many of these characters was neither simply family, marriage, nor adventure— the television staples. Instead, it was work, friendship, and romance in equal parts. And the target audience of the shows was the Pepsi generation, the Baby Boomers who made the word "life-style" part of the language. MTM had the vision to represent— possibly to anticipate—the tastes of these viewers, and made a fortune for Mary and Grant in the process. In 1974, MTM Enterprises employed some five hundred people and grossed $20 million.

In the second half of the 1970s, MTM suffered a creative slump. Fewer new shows were developed, and many of those that were just failed to click with audiences. Many industry observers wondered whether the MTM phenomenon had run out of steam when Jim Brooks and three other writers from *Mary Tyler*

Moore left MTM en masse for Paramount studios, where they worked on projects for ABC. Brooks says that there were growing tensions between the writers and the accountants at MTM. "One of the things that made MTM unique in the beginning is that the creative people—the writers—were put in charge; they even got to hire the business people," he says. "But as the company got bigger, Grant had to listen more to the business people. . . . He lost contact with some of his creative people." He attributes his move, though, to the fact that ABC offered him the opportunity to create, write, and produce a handful of series and specials without submitting pilots for approval. It was an offer he couldn't refuse.

Although he remained a consultant on shows like *Lou Grant*, as did Brooks, Allan Burns had also withdrawn from MTM by 1978 to concentrate on writing movie scripts. "I like writing, and I was doing almost no writing near the end at MTM," he says. "I was too bogged down in the logistics of producing, casting, meetings, and rewrites of ideas I'd give to someone else and they'd screw up." He and Brooks also agree that it's sometimes impossible to keep reproducing an initial success indefinitely. "Success can be a matter of chemistry and fate," Brooks points out. "Sometimes you achieve it only by accident." The task of producing a whole stable of successful shows in the *Mary Tyler Moore* mold led to a considerable amount of burnout among staff members.

Whatever the causes of the slump in MTM's ascendancy—whether it was a case of trying to do too much too soon, or the tail of profits wagging the dog of creativity, or simply the need for a new set of writers, producers, and ideas to come along—by the end of the decade MTM was ready to pull another rabbit out of the hat and start a new cycle of success.

Hill Street Blues debuted on NBC in January 1981. Network president Fred Silverman, having boosted ABC to first place, was trying to pull off the same trick for NBC. He asked MTM Enterprises for a shoot-'em-up cop drama set in "Fort Apache, the Bronx." What he got was a show unlike anything TV had seen before. *The Atlantic Monthly* has called *Hill Street* "a powerful synthesis of *Naked City*, *Dallas*, *The Edge of Night*, and *Dragnet*." Reviewers raved over its gritty look, due in part to the use of a hand-held camera, and its format, composed of three or four interlocking story lines that ran over several episodes each. Audience response, however, was a little slower off the mark.

At the end of its first season, *Hill Street* was so low in the ratings that it looked like a prime candidate for the chopping block. But when it swept the Emmy ceremony with an unheard-of eight awards, NBC crowed over its dedication to high-quality programming and gleefully renewed the series. Furthermore, audience research showed that while *Hill Street*'s following wasn't large, it was composed of a powerful segment of the population: professionals, property owners, and managers, or POMs, as they're called in the industry. These affluent, well-educated viewers are just the consumers that certain advertisers like to reach; *Hill Street* was the first television series ever to receive a long-term advertising commitment from Mercedes-Benz.

The audience grew noticeably during the show's second season. So important had *Hill Street* become, in fact, that MTM took pains to associate another new show with this established success in 1982. The new series was *St. Elsewhere*, which did for doctors and hospitals what *Hill Street* had done for cops and the South Bronx. Both shows revel in exploring their characters' weaknesses and failures as well as their successes, as is only appropriate in the Age of Analysis. Both manage to combine comedy and drama, character development and action, style and substance, campy humor and sincere emotion. But MTM's *Bay City Blues*, an attempt to extend the winning formula to a baseball team, failed disastrously and was canceled by NBC after just four episodes in the 1983–84 season.

For the sophisticated viewer who wants his light-hearted action laced with more liberal wit and romance (and a touch of *Dynasty*-type glitz) MTM offers *Remington Steele*, starring the suave Pierce Brosnan and Stephanie Zimbalist, his partner in crime-solving, verbal sparring, and smooching.

MTM Enterprises has been one of the most successful independent production companies ever to develop television series. In some years, MTM had more shows on all three networks than Paramount or Universal. But MTM has also branched out into other projects. The studio was the first commercial company to offer a series to public television: *Going Home Again*, a dramatic series about the lives of wealthy Californians in the years after Kennedy's assassination. Unfortunately, the Corporation for Public Broadcasting couldn't meet MTM's high overhead and the deal fell through.

Made-for-TV movies are a natural for a television production company, and MTM has made a handful of them, including several that were vehicles for Mary; one of them was an original for the pay-cable HBO network. Indeed, some industry observers have speculated that MTM, with its emphasis on production quality and yuppie demographics, will move into the cable market. The company hired a cable-TV marketing expert in 1983 to develop projects for pay TV. Nothing came of the attempt, and the expert's services were soon dispensed with, but the possibility remains open that MTM will develop and market cable-TV products in the near future.

The studio has also ventured into the volatile theatrical-movie market. In 1982, MTM produced a contemporary, mildly risqué romance called *A Little Sex*, starring Tim Matheson (*Animal House*) and Kate Capshaw (who later appeared in *Indiana Jones and the Temple of Doom*). Directed by *St. Elsewhere*'s executive producer, Bruce Paltrow, the movie did poorly at the box office but won favor with cable audiences before appearing on television in a badly dubbed version, which pointlessly changed all references to "sex" to "love." Although further movie ventures may follow, an MTM spokesman says the studio will continue to work on gaining space on the prime-time network schedules—still the best way to speak to Mass America.

What has all this meant to Mary?

For one thing, obviously, it has made her a very wealthy woman. Should she decide to retire today and never work again, she could go for the rest of her life without worrying about balancing her checkbook. But money has never been the primary reward for Mary.

MTM Enterprises has also made her powerful, one of Hollywood's "Queens of Clout," as a gossip columnist recently put it. As chairman of a powerful studio, she always gets a hearing when she has something to say within the industry. The studio developed and supported not just *Mary Tyler Moore* but Mary's reputation along with it. MTM has been good for Mary. But it has never been *hers*.

Mary is chairman of the board of MTM Enterprises, but the board she heads has reputedly met only twice in fifteen years. She doesn't even maintain an office at the company's headquarters. "Mary doesn't try to take over this desk and I don't try to tell her how to act," Grant Tinker said when he was president of MTM. And Mary remarked rather bitterly that "in much the same way that some men name a boat after their wives, he named the company after me, but that's the end of my involvement."

In 1981, Mary confided to Andy Warhol that she wanted to become more involved with MTM "as time goes on, to surround myself with people who know what they're doing." Mary now has a huge staff running MTM for her, and Grant is no longer president of the studio. She has been involved in a number of recent MTM projects. Although she has never been interested in management, in the day-to-day business of running a company, it's conceivable that Mary might choose to take a more active role in the creative work of the studio—writing, directing, or producing—as well as acting. One thing is certain: she has the means at her disposal to try anything she wants to do. Like MTM Enterprises, Mary is a sweet kitten with a powerful roar. If the lion is the king of the jungle, she is definitely one of the queens of show biz.

Nothing Is Forever

Riding high in the ratings in the early 1970s, Mary appeared to have it all.

She was established as a star of the first magnitude, with a series of her own designed to showcase her talent to its best advantage. High ratings and numerous awards documented her success. Best of all, she loved doing the show—it made up for the years as second banana on *Dick Van Dyke* and for her failures and disappointments on the stage and the movie screen.

After the doubts and disasters of the post–Van Dyke years, Mary had vindicated herself. She had turned the tables on critics who claimed that her success as Laura Petrie had been a fluke, or that she had ridden to success on Dick Van Dyke's talent. And if she had ever harbored such fears herself, she now knew that they were groundless.

Home for Mary and Grant during these years was a modest (by Hollywood standards, of course) mansion on Beverly Drive—one of the most posh streets in Beverly Hills. Grant had his Cadillac, Mary had her Jaguar XKE, and together they accumulated a respectable collection of art. Although Richie, now in his early teens, spent a lot of time with his father in Fresno, three dogs kept the Tinker residence from being *too* quiet. Their pets may have sported the aristocratic names of Maud, Diswilliam, and Maxim de Winter (the last named after the hero of Daphne du Maurier's *Rebecca*), but Mary kept insisting that the Tinkers were really "barefoot people." They were becoming powerful and respected in the entertainment community, but there was also something just a little bit dull about them—they had a middle-American quality that didn't strike many sparks in the Hollywood social scene. They didn't go out much, and they never made it to the "A-list" parties.

Mary's favorite spare-time activities weren't shopping on Rodeo Drive and having affairs with other celebrities, but needlepoint and barbecues. And although the distinguished Grant Tinker never appeared in public looking anything but impeccably groomed, Mary claimed that "he's happier in a sweat shirt and Levi's than anybody." She was even building a big house on the beach at Malibu for them.

Meanwhile, Grant left Twentieth Century–Fox to devote himself full-time to managing MTM Enterprises—and MTM herself. So Mary had a loving, protective husband whom she described as her "guide, mentor, and primary decision-maker," and said more than once that without him, "I do not function." Remarks like these, coupled with Grant's well-known direction of his wife's career, gradually built up a picture of a marriage clearly dominated by the husband. And Mary seemed to like it that way. She once said to an interviewer that although she knew the women's lib faction would not approve, she herself felt that the husband should have the stronger voice in a marriage. "I know there are people who say marriage should be fifty-fifty," she remarked, "but I think seventy-five–one hundred is really the way it should be."

In short, Mary had what looked from the outside like the perfect job, the perfect marriage, and the perfect home life. But while the job continued to go smoothly, everything else somehow began to fall apart.

First came trouble with Richie. Sadly, the two had never been close. It is an axiom of psychology that people reproduce the behavior of their parents, and it is indicative of her father's importance in Mary's life that her problems with Richie mirrored her father's problems with her. Mary now had a chance to play Daddy's role—after all, Grant was Richie's stepfather, so Mary was his primary parent. And, tragically, Mary had as much difficulty communicating with Richie as her father had had communicating with her.

She had tried to make time for him during the various stages of her career, but it is easy to believe that he might have seen himself as a bit player in her life. Her commitment to acting, her very public statements that being a housewife, stuck at home all day, was not the life for her—all this must have made Richie feel that he had little to share with his mother. Combined with the normal rebelliousness of adolescence, his resentment of the Tinkers' way of life was enough to drive him out of their house.

As he grew older, Richie spent more and more time with his father. Then, in 1973, when Richie was seventeen, he left Mary and Grant to live with his father and his stepmother, Jeanette, in Fresno. To his classmates at Bullard High, he was a "natural athlete" and a "free spirit." But Mary quarreled with him over his grades (which were as bad as hers had been), his dabbling in drugs, and even the hideous tattoo he displayed during a visit to the set—for that one, she broke a longtime rule and blasted him in public.

"He was a child of the Sixties," Mary says. "It wasn't an easy time to grow up. He went through a period of distrusting anyone who had money. He thought it would be really nifty to live in a house where you had to make your own bed and wash the dishes. He rebelled against my affluence.

"And I saw his point," she continues. "You do get closer to your kids when you have to pull together for survival. I'm not saying poverty is great, but maybe something in between lots of money and no money at all. . . ." But Mary and Richie weren't able to draw together over soapsuds and bed-making. Richie was now in Fresno. Communication between the two was poor and infrequent, and their relationship would worsen over the next few years.

Then, as if to suggest that at this point in her life Mary wasn't capable of hanging on to any important relationship, her marriage deteriorated. Neither Grant nor Mary has ever pinpointed the source of the trouble, but it is obvious that the relationship had gone stale for both of them. Married life began to seem rather unfulfilling to Mary. "I'd get home at six o'clock and wait for Grant," she says. "I'd read or study my script, put new ribbons on my ballet shoes, and do other things to keep busy. I didn't have a lot of girlfriends. Not too many outlets. In fact, I had so few spheres of interest, there wasn't much brought into our marriage," she admits. Grant was also involved in his work to the exclusion of other interests or activities, and finally they realized that they had a problem instead of a working marriage.

"We began to take one another for granted," Mary says. "When we began building our new home at the beach, we never really discussed how we felt about living there." Grant adds, "I thought Mary wanted to live at the beach, and she thought I did. Actually, neither of us really wanted to live way out there." The beach house was an expensive symbol of the communication that had gone sadly awry between Mary and Grant, just as it had between Mary and Richie. And around the time Richie moved to Fresno, Grant also moved out of the new house Mary had built and into an apartment of his own. They had been married for eleven years.

Mary claims that they discussed the separation and its effect on their work and decided that although they'd be only a hundred yards apart in the MTM studio, they wouldn't see each other. The separation took place on a Friday, the day Mary's show was due to be taped. "I had heard rumors," says Treva Silverman, at the time a senior story consultant on *MTM*, "and when Grant didn't show up in the control room that Friday night for the filming, we knew. The tension was just awful, but Mary was wonderful on the stage. I don't know how she did it." It was the first filming Grant had missed since his wife's series began.

"I'll never forget that day," says Dan Jenkins, who was Mary's public relations man. "That afternoon, Mary had to entertain some British journalists. One of them leaned over to her at the end of lunch and said, 'Tell me, Mary, how is it that you have such a *marvelous* marriage?' Well, Mary gave all the right answers, but when she got up to leave I could see her put her hand to her mouth, kind of choking back a sob." The incident epitomizes Mary's stern self-control—she could give the British lessons in the "stiff upper lip" attitude any day.

Suddenly Mary Tyler Moore, like Mary Richards, was single—at least temporarily. However, the real-life Mary didn't meet the occasion with quite the resourcefulness or "spunk" that Mary Richards might have shown. Mary Richards, for example, might have found some help, or at least comfort, in talking over her confusion and anxiety with Rhoda or Lou. But Mary led a solitary life, like a lonely princess in her Malibu palace. She admitted that Grant was more than her best friend. He was her only friend. And at this crisis in her personal life she made no move to develop new friends or to become closer to any of her many acquaintances. Nor did she turn to her own family for support.

Instead, she flung herself at her work, as if to anesthetize her pain with long hours and repeated rehearsals. Perhaps she needed to prove to herself that although her marriage was on the rocks, she could still be perfect at *something*. Alone at home at night, she walked the beach or wrote page after page in her diary. She spent a lonely Christmas in Puerto

Rico. And after six weeks, she and Grant began to draw together again.

That they loved each other is undeniable. It's also possible, though, that Mary reunited with Grant so quickly because she didn't want to be alone and had no other direction to take. Certainly there was no other man in her life. Her protective husband and rigorous schedule had insulated her from even innocent relationships with men. Although the rumor spread that she was involved with Jim Brooks, it was based on nothing more than mutual affection and his sympathy for her during the separation, which he expressed with a hug after a particularly hard day filming the episode about Ed Asner's divorce.

However it happened, Grant and Mary began "dating." Both expressed some doubts that the romance could ever return to their relationship, but they spent time together anyway and, says Mary, those dates "struck a responsive chord in me. There *was* a romantic element involved, and I welcomed it. I was very excited, very careful about wearing the right thing." They started spending more and more nights together—at Grant's apartment in town, *not* at the beach house—and eventually they set up housekeeping again and moved into a big house in Bel Air. And they gave cheerful interviews to the press, in which they explained what a good idea it is for couples to separate periodically to reevaluate their relationships. The split ended as satisfactorily as if it had been written into a sitcom. But there's really no such thing as a "happy separation." For six weeks, Mary had been unhappy and adrift, and she was now aware that both she and Grant would have to work to keep their marriage alive, not just coast along and hope that it would magically take care of itself.

Before, during, and after Mary and Grant's separation, *Mary Tyler Moore* continued to sail along, an unqualified success. "Mary's is the kind of show that keeps vice-presidents of programming happy," said a beaming Perry Lafferty, who held that position at CBS. "It has no problems whatsoever."

Even hyperintellectual types, the sort of people who say proudly, "Oh, I never watch TV," developed a sneaking fondness for the show. A *New York Times* writer said, "Mary is so In, actually, that it has become especially fashionable to drift into the den at a party—or even go home—at nine on Saturday night because you simply 'must not miss' her program." Mary even appeared in a cartoon in *The New Yorker*—a hallmark of urbane wit. To the delight of millions, she went on giving awful parties, coping gracefully with a declaration of love from coworker Murray, unintentionally cracking up at the funeral of Chuckles the Clown, sneaking a furtive peek at herself in the mirror on the bedroom ceiling of manhunter Sue Ann Nivens, the Happy Homemaker, or gently but pointedly deflating Ted Baxter's ego whenever he became particularly intolerable. After Phyllis left, she got a new apartment and a new neighbor, Paula Kovacs, played by Penny Marshall. But the chemistry that had sparked Mary's friendship with Rhoda was missing, and Paula vanished after one season.

Off-screen the *MTM* ensemble was, in many ways, one big happy family, like the *Dick Van Dyke* crew. Mary was noted for her graciousness to TV newcomers like Georgia Engel, who played Ted's fluff-brained girlfriend, and to visiting performers, like the men who portrayed her string of inconclusive boy-friends. After all, she hadn't forgotten how nervous she'd been as a newcomer herself on *Dick Van Dyke*. "There I was," she recalled, "surrounded by all those pros and hoping I wouldn't miss my mark, or ruin my makeup, or forget my lines. Georgia reminded me of *me*. She was trying so hard and she was really very, very good. Right from the start, her timing was impeccable, and the way she delivered her lines in that wispy, little-girl voice of hers just knocked us all out."

Mary organized a daily hour-long dance and aero-bics class for the women on the set. Attendance was optional, of course . . . and they all attended. Valerie Harper credits these sessions with helping her lose thirty pounds over her years upstairs from Mary. But while the atmosphere at *MTM* was pleasant, it was also businesslike and highly professional, and a bit impersonal. Mary seldom exerted her authority or lost her temper—but everyone knew that the author-ity and the temper were there in reserve.

Although the show was shot in Los Angeles, Mary, Grant, Valerie Harper, and other members of the cast and crew occasionally visited Minneapolis to shoot location scenes and new bits for the show's opening credits—like the shot that shows Mary feeding ducks in the city's Loring Park. These visits generated a lot of excitement in the locals, who were proud to have their city featured in one of the country's top shows. Mary even received a plaque from Governor Wendell R. Anderson, thanking her for her endorsement of the city as a great place to live. A businessman whose work caused him to meet a number of people from the Minneapolis–St. Paul area noted years later that the city's residents were still proud of the show, and speculated that *MTM* had noticeably improved the self-esteem of midwesterners. And a Minnesota housewife who was working on her first novel, which would someday be called *Ordinary People*, included "the house that Mary Richards lived in" whenever she had a chance to show visitors the sights of Minneapolis.

Members of the ensemble were free to work on other projects, of course. Cloris Leachman won an Oscar for her supporting actress role in *The Last Picture Show* in 1971, and Ed Asner scored Emmys for his television work in *Rich Man, Poor Man* and *Roots.* Mary herself became involved in several "on the side" projects—one of which took her to Russia.

First, Mary flexed her MTM Enterprises muscles to get what she had always wanted—a chance to prove herself as a dancer. In January 1976, CBS aired an hour-long special starring Mary and a supporting cast of singers and dancers, including Ben Vereen. Originally called "The Creation of the Universe and the History of the World as Seen by Mary Tyler Moore in an Hour," it was mercifully retitled "Mary's Incredible Dream." Consisting entirely of songs and dances—thirty of them in a row—it gave Mary the chance to strut her stuff in tights, gowns, and a variety of costumes and dance styles. Unfortunately for Mary, however, the only thing that turned out to be incredible about "Mary's Incredible Dream" was its incredibly bad ratings.

But Mary's well-known devotion to dance wasn't

tempered by this disaster. Later that year, Mary was asked by CBS producer Alvin Cooperman to host a special celebrating the bicentennial of the U.S.S.R.'s famous Bolshoi Ballet.

"The Bolshoi Ballet: Romeo and Juliet" was an unusual production. For one thing, many observers found it odd to celebrate the bicentennial of a Russian organization in America's own bicentennial year, particularly as the show was scheduled to air just one week before July 4. Cooperman justified this by saying, "I don't think it cuts into our own celebration. If anything, it's an enhancement—a salute to our bicentennial from an institution of similar age." For another, the show wasn't really a CBS production. It was put together as a joint venture by the Russians, the West Germans, and the British Broadcasting Company. CBS simply obtained rights to the American version. The bicentennial performance in Moscow was aired in 115 countries, and Mary appeared as hostess only in the American program. (The British hostess was to be former ballerina Beryl Grey.) Mary's role was limited to opening and closing remarks and a brief interview between acts of the ballet, and she was dressed in a gown throughout, not in a dancer's leotard and tutu.

Still, it was an exciting project for Mary, as well as a public vindication of her image as a dancer—or at least a person who knew something about dance. She has always cared deeply about the great ballet companies of the world. In fact, she says, one of her favorite memories is of an experience that took place while she was in London, filming *Run a Crooked Mile*. "The show's public-relations lady knew I was a dance fanatic and also knew that the ballet master of the Royal Ballet was a *Dick Van Dyke Show* fan," she recalls. She was invited to exercise at the barre of the Royal Ballet. "It was one of the highlights of my life. The first day I walked in, one girl asked, 'Are you new to the company?' Boy, was I flattered!" So naturally Mary's response to Cooperman's offer was, "I love it, I love it!"

The shooting schedule called for Mary to visit Moscow at the coldest time of the Russian year, in January. She was there for seven very busy days. Grant accompanied her. No sooner had they recovered from jet lag than they attended a party given by Richard Roth, a correspondent for CBS News. They feasted on vodka and caviar and gossiped about the surprise visit of Henry Kissinger, who wasn't at the party but was in Moscow. The next day's party was hosted by Ambassador Walter Sloessel at the U.S. embassy. Then Grant and Mary endured a long train ride and a blizzard to visit the Hermitage, the spectacular Leningrad art museum that houses paintings by Picasso, Cézanne, and Gauguin, among others. They returned to Moscow tired and behind schedule, but taping for the special began at once.

Work had to be done during intermissions, so it proceeded with many interruptions, not as smoothly as Mary was accustomed to. Grant had to be commandeered to hold her cue cards, and once they were interrupted by a gang of mop-wielding cleaning women, who insisted on finishing their job before the taping could proceed. Mary even had to turn down an invitation to join Kissinger in his box—she was too busy with the hectic situation backstage. But finally the obstacles were overcome and Mary's task was complete, including the first interview in fifteen years with the company's ballet mistress and grande dame, Galina Ulanova, who had created the role of Juliet many years before.

As proud as she was to do the show, Mary was glad to be back in the U.S.A. Several things about her Russian experience had left her feeling critical. One was the Tinkers' accommodations in Moscow's new Intourist Hotel: a two-room apartment with no bathroom or closets—"they pounded a nail into the wall to hang up my evening gowns," she said later. Another was the way she was manhandled by a soldier: "He grabbed my arm and tried to pull me away from a doorway of the theater when we were filming the opening of the show. He barked something that didn't need any interpretation. I tried to point out that we were filming, but he couldn't have cared less." She reflected, "I don't want to be thought of as an ugly American or a flag-waver, but the trip certainly made me glad to be living under our system— our faults notwithstanding." As an actress who was used to getting what she wanted promptly and with no questions asked, Mary found the Red red tape particularly frustrating.

But she loved the experience of the ballet, which she called "the universal language of dance." And she was impressed by the Soviet Union's commitment to and support of the arts, citing the fact that the Bolshoi keeps even the older members of the troupe under contract. "We use a young dancer made up to look like an older character," she mused. "They use a sixty-five-year-old dancer who fits the part." Mary says that she almost caused an international incident, too. "While waiting to talk to Ulanova, I sat in Plisetskaya's dressing room. [Plisetskaya was one of the leading stars of the Bolshoi.] Her ballet slippers were in an open drawer. I had to fight the urge to take one as a souvenir." Fortunately for détente, Mary resisted temptation and came home without her souvenir.

Even before Mary went to Russia, she had made a decision that stunned and saddened TV watchers. She announced that the 1976–77 season, the show's seventh, would be the last for *Mary Tyler Moore*. "One more season beyond this and then good-bye," she said. "Nothing is forever."

11

Lights Out

The next few years were to be agonizingly difficult ones for Mary, bringing her deepest personal challenges. Unexpected triumphs and grievous tragedies followed close on one another's heels.

She had loved every minute of her years as Mary Richards, Mary said, but at this point in her career she was beginning to feel the urge to spread her wings a little wider. Occasional specials weren't what she wanted. In fact, she wasn't altogether sure what she *did* want, except she hoped that it would allow her to dance and she was pretty sure it would involve the medium of television. So that meant saying goodbye to Mary Richards. "If having a career means having to play the same character for the rest of my life," she said, "then I would choose not to have a career. It would be so stultifying." Perhaps she was beginning to be bored with Mary Richards, too, after 168 episodes. But she was very proud of what the show had achieved.

"It's made people laugh at things that also made them think," she claimed. "It has, apparently, made an awful lot of women who had been ashamed of being alone and dateless on Saturday nights suddenly very happy with themselves, content to be alone. I don't mean to imply for a moment that Mary Richards could ever take the place of sex . . . but at least it stopped a source of guilt and tremendous worry for an awful lot of people on Saturdays." Mary was also proud of the fact that her show had been the first in television to hire a woman—Treva Silverman—as a senior story consultant, and the first to star a single woman who was neither man-hungry nor old-maidish, just normal.

Like Dick Van Dyke and a very few other television performers before her, Mary was wise enough to quit while she was ahead. She ended her series gracefully and with style, not waiting for time, the audiences, or the sponsors to end it for her. "In seven years, we explored every situation that was natural to Mary as we had created her," she acknowledged. "To continue, we would have had to either change Mary's life in some way, such as having her get married, which we didn't want to do because we thought audiences wouldn't like it, or start repeating ourselves. So it was time to quit." On this occasion, Mary's sense of timing served her well. Every episode of the show remains fresh and vital, and it left the air to a chorus of laments.

Because the decision to end the series was made well in advance, there was plenty of time for a special closing show to be written. Most critics and fans agree that it was one of the best of the series. As Mary said, "It's a show about saying good-bye," and it was at once charming, funny, and very poignant. It was filmed before a closed audience that contained neither the press nor the public, just three hundred "close friends of the show." The episode involved the purchase of WJM by a new owner. He promises to make big changes, and everybody assumes that Ted will be fired. He calls the staff into his office—and fires all but Ted. At home, Mary receives a surprise visit from Rhoda and Phyllis, but even this fails to cheer her up—especially as they bicker with one another just as much as they did when she first met them seven years ago. In the final scene, Mary, Lou, Murray, and Ted say good-bye in the newsroom, joining in a group hug that perfectly distills the show's magical blend of humor and sentiment. Then they file out one by one. The last to leave, Mary comes back into the deserted room a moment later and turns off the lights for the last time.

"It was the strangest acting I've ever done," Mary said afterward. "The script called for us all to play the exact emotions we were actually feeling—all saying good-bye to one another for the last time. Actors usually have to work hard to dredge up deep emotion. This time I had to fight that emotion to hold back the tears. When you cry, it's not very pretty or intelligible. But I wept, and so did every member of the cast. The audience gave us a standing ovation, then I introduced the cast and writers one at a time. I was so emotionally shaken I could hardly pronounce their names as they took their bows. It was really a gripping moment, and my tears were very real."

Each cast member took away something from the set as a memento. Mary took the gold "M" that used to hang on the wall of her apartment.

Mary Richards left prime-time on March 19, 1977,

and made her way into syndicated reruns all over the country. *MTM* has remained one of the most popular syndications ever since. In fact, for many months large numbers of New Yorkers coped with night-owl schedules in order to watch the three segments that appeared between two-thirty and four A.M. But while her fictional namesake went on throwing parties and throwing her hat into the air over and over again, the real Mary looked around for something to do.

Earlier, she had spoken of taking a year off, to rest, relax, and recharge her batteries. But long before a year had passed, Mary was tired of resting and rarin' to go. But in what direction?

CBS wanted her to start a new comedy series immediately. But, still caught up in her lifelong dream of being a dancer, Mary was determined that her next TV series would be a variety show, with lots of singing and toe tapping. She resumed her dance lessons and threw in voice lessons on the side. In the meantime, however, Grant had suggested a project that Mary was very eager to do.

He suggested that MTM Enterprises feature Mary in a television movie based on Betty Rollin's bestseller, *First, You Cry*. It would turn out to be an exciting change of pace for Mary. In 1974, Betty Rollin, a new correspondent for NBC, had discovered a malignant tumor in her breast. Ironically, the discovery came just months after she had completed a news special on breast cancer, focusing on Betty Ford's recent mastectomy. Rollin underwent an operation that left her without a left breast. *First, You Cry* chronicled her feelings about the operation as well as the radical changes that it brought about in her personal and professional life.

Mary was deeply moved by *First, You Cry.* "I felt after reading it that if it ever happened to me or to somebody close to me, I would handle it much better," she says, possibly remembering her anguish at discovering that she had diabetes and her struggles to come to grips with the disease. "I wanted to reach as many people as possible with the show. I cared very much about this project. This is a subject of concern not only to every woman alive but also to every man with a mother, sister, or lover."

Rollin did not write the screenplay for the movie; it was written by Carmen Culver. In fact, Rollin was scarcely involved in the production at all, except to visit the set once in New York and twice in Los Angeles. "She brought her mother," Mary remembers, "and in New York she introduced me to her ex-husband, Arthur Herzog." Herzog was portrayed in the film by Tony Perkins, of *Psycho* fame. Rollin claimed that she had faith in Mary and in producer Philip Barry and director George Schaefer to do justice to her story.

Mary was delighted to be working again, and in a project that stretched her abilities. "This is the first character I've played without relying on my personal bag of tricks," she said. "We all have them, especially those of us who have been in comedy a certain amount of time. It was kind of difficult for me not to be Laura Petrie or Mary Richards or even Mary Tyler Moore."

Perhaps Mary took on *First, You Cry* in order to prove to the critics and to herself that she could handle a full-length dramtic role—she may even have hoped that her movie career would be revived by it, although she denied this; perhaps she realized that, at forty, she could no longer play the lighthearted ingenue and wanted to appear publicly in a part that would help lay the ghosts of Laura Petrie and Mary Richards. Or perhaps she simply wanted to exercise some long-unused feelings in a very emotional script.

"It's emotionally wrenching, not just because of Betty's mastectomy, but because of her inability to deal with various aspects of her life, including a marriage that wasn't working out. There are moments of high drama and weepy scenes that, thanks to George Schaefer, come off very well," she said shortly before the movie aired. "I don't think I embarrassed myself as an actress."

Tragically, Mary suffered an emotionally wrenching experience of her own while *First, You Cry* was being filmed on location in New York. Her twenty-one-year-old sister, Elizabeth Ann Moore, killed herself with a drug overdose in Los Angeles.

Elizabeth was only three months older than Richie. Because Mary had been leading a busy, turbulent life on her own while Elizabeth was growing up, the two had never been close. But siblings separated by many years often draw closer together as they grow older and the age difference becomes less significant. Mary and Elizabeth were not to have that chance.

Mary and Grant immediately flew out from New York, in a state of shock. The press speculated as to whether Elizabeth's death was suicide or accident. Mary was too appalled to say anything, and Grant told interviewers curtly, "It's a private family matter." Mary's Aunt Bertie, who had sheltered her when she was a teenager with problems, said, "The poor girl died of a heart seizure. Can't you leave it at that?" But the official coroner's report of the autopsy revealed "pulmonary edema, a condition that is consistent with a person who has taken an overdose."

Eventually, the facts surrounding Elizabeth's death came to light. A student at Los Angeles City College, with a part-time job at KNXT-TV (Aunt Bertie's old station), Elizabeth led a troubled love life. "She was going with a young man," Mary said, "and the relationship was coming to an end. She was sedating herself, taking Darvon, and she took too many and she also had two drinks that night and—she died. That's the story of that. She was a wonderful, wonderful girl and she was not a drug taker." But the private doubts and uncertainties that Mary must have felt can only have made the bitter waste of her young sister's life even more difficult to bear.

Back in New York, Mary went back to work on *First, You Cry*, which was scheduled to be broadcast in November. In February 1978, just a week after her sister's funeral, she suffered another loss—this time of professional prestige. Her second hour-long variety special was aired. Called "How to Survive the Seventies and Maybe Even Bump into Happiness" (where did these long titles come from, anyway?), it bombed. The only thing it bumped into was the bottom of the ratings chart, and it didn't survive the manhandling it took from the critics. Even *The Carol Burnett Show*'s Harvey Korman and *Three's Company*'s John Ritter couldn't add much gusto to the lackluster assemblage of skits and spoofs. It was a good sign that without a strong character that she could play well, Mary wasn't really capable of pulling a show together. Her low-key humor was ill-suited to satire and didn't satisfy an audience who was waiting to howl at John Belushi as a killer bee.

Despite this discouraging omen, however, Mary decided that year to come back to television in the new series CBS had promised her—and she insisted on making it an hour-long variety show. She claimed over and over again that she needed the artistic challenge of doing a show that wasn't a sitcom. But certain other comments hint at a strain of real masochism in her determination to prove herself a musical variety star after two spectacular duds. She claimed that *Mary Tyler Moore* had stopped being "frightening" enough for her. "I missed being scared," she said. "Worrying is part of my nature. You need challenges, fears, uncertainty, a certain amount of crying at night." Her two specials undoubtedly told Mary that doing a variety show would give her plenty to cry about, yet she persisted in her plan.

All this was taking place at a time when the variety show, like the dinosaur, was dying off and being replaced by smaller, quicker creatures. One reason for this may be found in audience demographics. Maybe stars like Jackie Gleason and Dinah Shore had been successful with variety shows in the 1950s and 1960s, when families watched TV together, because they offered wholesome, innocuous entertainment with a little something for everybody. But in the 1970s, with the death of the nuclear family bemoaned daily, there were more splinter households and viewers who had special tastes and wanted shows that were all comedy, all crime, all adventure, all whatever.

Television shows, in fact, were becoming something like radio stations, where a listener tunes in to his or her specialty and nothing else, be it acid rock or Bach cantatas. Variety shows were too much like those easy-listening stations heard only in office buildings and elevators. Only Carol Burnett was keeping hers alive. The list of entertainers who had failed at variety shows in the 1970s included both luminaries and lightweights: Leslie Uggams, the Captain and Tennille, Tim Conway, Mac Davis, Bobbie Gentry, Julie Andrews, Tony Orlando and Dawn, and more. Most of these were singers, and they bombed anyway. But Mary, who had never really established herself as a singer or dancer, was eager to rush in where the more cautious programming executives may have feared to tread.

Mary had been promised a series, however, and they gave her what she wanted. MTM veterans Tom Patchett and Jay Tarses, who had worked on *MTM* and *The Bob Newhart Show*, came up with *Mary*. Mary herself had vetoed the idea of guest stars—perhaps fearing that they might eclipse her in a medium she knew would be tricky for her?—so they surrounded her with even more regulars than Carol Burnett had on her show. There were six of them: David Letterman, Michael Keaton, Dick Shawn, James Hampton, Swoosie Kurtz, and Judy Kahan. As usual with the ensembles picked by MTM Enterprises, they were a talented bunch, most of whom have gone on to successes of their own. The trouble was that there were too many of them on *Mary*, resulting in a cluttered, overly busy quality to which virtually every reviewer objected. The plan was that together this mob would present a mixed menu of songs, dances, comedy skits, and satire. Typical of the material they were given to work with was the "Date of the Week" segment. On each show, Mary would go out with "a bigger and funnier loser than the week before." Well, maybe Mary Richards could turn a disastrous date into a joke, but somehow when the real Mary (now forty-one) did it, it seemed sad rather than funny— and cruel, too, which Mary Richards had never been. Another segment of the series premiere was a production number by "The Ed Asner Dancers," a group of large men who lumbered about with Mary. Unfortunately, the humor was as heavy as their feet.

Mary underwent the predictable comparisons with Carol Burnett. "Unlike Burnett, Mary's not a natural comedienne, who can stand up there and create humor as she goes along," said one critic. Another said, "Now Mary knows what her old costar Dick Van Dyke went through when he floundered after the demise of his successful CBS series."

The show just didn't come together. In its favor it can be said that it was a new venture, with new talent, and it might well have improved—after all, *The Dick Van Dyke Show* wasn't a hit in its first season, but it picked up an audience over time. But *Mary* wasn't given time. The premiere was blasted out of the sky in the ratings by *Battlestar Galactica* and *Centennial*. By the third show, *Mary*'s audience share was only 24 percent, but 30 percent is usually regarded as the minimum a show needs to survive. In a move that startled reviewers by its abruptness, CBS announced after only three shows had been aired that it was yanking *Mary*. Eleven shows were in the can, but not even the one scheduled for the fourth week would be shown. Instead, the network juggled *All in the Family*, *Alice*, and a special Sunday-night showing of *Dallas* to fill the time slot. The move was so sudden that the show was history even before some promotional interviews with Mary had made it into print.

The cancellation of *Mary* and the events that followed kept the Hollywood gossip mill busy for months. First of all, there was a rumor that CBS had deliberately put *Mary* in an unsuitable time slot—nine P.M. on Sunday, opposite strong competition. Mary made a point of telling interviewers, "Oh, no, we asked for this Sunday-night period. We wanted to follow directly after *60 Minutes* because we think that audience is exactly the right audience for our show." Two months before the show was due to premiere, she explained blithely, "The one thing we know about the audience that watches *60 Minutes* is that it's wide-awake, and you can't say that for all audiences. And our kind of show will require some attention. You know, it's not going to be frothy. It's going to be easy to watch, but we're going to be doing grown-up material. And we want a grown-up audience."

Mary may have been serious, but to reviewers who wondered whether wide-awake concentration should really be necessary for a variety show and why Mary thought an audience tuned in for serious investigative journalism would stick around for lightweight laughs, her explanation sounded hollow. Some thought that she was making the best of what she knew to be a bad situation. Mary had always been given star treatment by CBS, but this time it looked as if the network either lacked confidence in her new show or wanted to put her drawing appeal to the acid test.

Rumors also abounded in the trade press that MTM, not CBS, had pulled the plug on *Mary*. One report said that while the network had been willing to move the show to a more favorable time slot, the studio had lost confidence in it and ordered it canceled. One reason for this might be to minimize the damage to Mary's reputation by not giving the show time to get worse; another might be to allow CBS to appear the villain. Contradictory stories flew around New York and Hollywood, and the matter was never publicly settled, but the end result was much the same no matter which side was responsible for taking the show off the air. In her third try at bat (counting the two earlier variety specials), Mary had struck out. Variety, it seemed, was just not destined to spice up her life.

When *Mary* was yanked, the relationship between CBS and MTM became even more strained. MTM held CBS to the letter of its twenty-two show contract, and the network agreed to schedule a new series for Mary as soon as it was ready. Mary immediately announced that she'd be back within months . . . with a *new* variety show. And although the network loyally backed her up in press releases and public statements, some industry watchers began to say that Mary's insistence on working in a format that had already failed for her three times was not only doomed to disaster but also more than a little bit obsessive. Perhaps those inspiring movie musicals of the 1930s and 1940s, those gallant tap-dancing heroines who had given Mary so much inspiration and idealism, were haunting her too persistently. She seemed unable to give up her childhood dreams, even though she risked irreparable harm to her television reputation if she bombed again. So development and production got under way for her second hour-long variety show in less than six months.

But in the not-too-tranquil lull between the death of *Mary* and the birth pangs of its successor, Mary reaped the rewards of her earlier willingness to try something bold and new. *First, You Cry* was shown in November 1978 to great acclaim.

The production had weak spots, notably in Tony Perkins, as Rollin's husband, and Richard Crenna, as the man she has an affair with after her marriage falls apart. But reviewers and the audience alike responded to its compassionate, full-blooded attempt to show that the story of a woman with a cancer is *not* just the story of the cancer. "*First, You Cry* is simply the personal story of one rather special case," as the *New York Times* put it, adding, "Miss Moore makes it very much worth watching."

John J. O'Connor of the *Times* wasn't alone in praising Mary's performance. Even reviews and articles that didn't rave about the show as a whole singled out Mary's performance for commendation. Her good reviews, it is true, contained a rather large element of "Who would have believed that Little Miss Sunshine could play such a serious role so competently?" which may have exasperated Mary. But at the same time, she had set out to prove just that point.

The people who saw *First, You Cry* saw a new Mary Tyler Moore—an actress who, for the first time in her career, was able to create a character who wasn't the same as her real-life persona, however much she may have drawn upon her own suffering and wisdom to convey emotion. It is impossible to watch the deeply moving scene where she explores the scars left by the operation, for example, without believing that the woman on the screen is all too familiar with the body's betrayal and the fear and anguish it costs. Betty Rollin herself was pleased with what MTM and Mary had wrought; she wrote Mary "the most beautiful letter" to say so. O'Connor summed up his assessment of her thus: "The performance is strong, daring in some respects, and completely convincing." The following spring, Mary was nominated for an Emmy for best actress in a dramatic special, and the film was nominated in three other categories as well. Those accolades were some consolation when her new series flopped.

It was called *The Mary Tyler Moore Hour*, and it premiered in early 1979. Many viewers were confused, not knowing if it was another special, a continuation of her series from the previous fall, or something else entirely. It incorporated some changes. Personnel changes, among others. Mary scrapped the half-dozen regulars from her earlier show (except for Michael Keaton, who stayed on), and replaced them with just two: Joyce Van Patten and Michael Lombard. Veteran network executive Perry Lafferty, who had been in charge of programming *Mary Tyler Moore* during the 1970s, came in as producer, and the former production crew was replaced from top to bottom.

Possibly sensing grimly that this would be her last grab at the brass ring, Mary was leaving nothing to chance.

In addition, Mary had reversed her rule about guest stars, and the new series abounded with them: Lucille Ball, Gene Kelly, Erik Estrada, and more. Their presence was accounted for by the show's unwieldy format—MTM called it a "sitvar," a hybrid of sitcom and variety. The premise was that Mary, now called Mary McKinnon, is the star of a CBS weekly series. Mary Tyler Moore's weekly escapades would revolve around Mary McKinnon's weekly attempts to find a guest star for *her* show. . . . On the show's premiere, for example, Nancy Walker is unable to appear, so Mary tries to get Lucille Ball. She ambushes her in a famous Beverly Hills boutique, and the two women proceed to knock back Irish coffees until Lucy says yes. But Mary also has to get Mike Douglas's okay to release Lucy from her deal to cohost *his* show that day, and it goes on and on. The feeble plot does serve to link the various guest appearances together, but that's about all that can be said for it. Audiences had failed to respond to the show-within-a-show idea when Betty White tried it, and they didn't like it any better with Mary. In another bit of ill-advised gimmickry, MTM got hold of an old piece of film footage showing Stan Laurel and Oliver Hardy in one of their funny dance routines and spliced Mary into it. The problem was that the two funnymen made her look pretty poor by comparison.

The network was not quite as ruthless this time around. It let *The Mary Tyler Moore Hour* linger until

May before putting the show out of its misery. At which point Mary began to say that CBS had canceled her first variety series prematurely. "It was kind of a watered-down *Saturday Night Live*—offbeat humor, black humor, very sharp humor, and I don't think the audience was ready to see me in that setting," she said. "But I think it would have worked eventually had they not been gun-shy and taken it off." She also said that she "had never truly believed" that the second variety format, with its plot and guests, would work. One can only wonder why, if that is true, she continued with the project? Was she so obsessed with the notion of succeeding in a variety show that she couldn't turn back? Or was she now changing her story retroactively, with the 20/20 vision of hindsight?

Whatever the truth about the tortured ins and outs of Mary's ill-fated shows, one thing emerged from the fiasco. Mary finally realized that she simply wasn't cut out to make it doing what she had always wanted to do—singing, dancing, clowning around. She had run out of excuses for the shows and the audiences. It must have been very hard for her to let go of the dream that had cost her so much and had kept her in dance slippers for thirty-five years, but she announced to the press that she would never try a variety show again. "I think I've worked all that out of my system," she said, regretfully. She also remarked, a little bitterly, "As some journalist was kind enough to point out to me, why does a forty-year-old woman suddenly think she can become a song-and-dance man?"

That was as close as Mary came to taking the blame for the failures of *Mary* and *The Mary Tyler*

Moore Hour. For the most part, she accounted for them to the press by saying, "Things in the entertainment world go in cycles, and that was a period when variety shows just weren't popular with the public."

CBS paid off its contract with Mary, rumored to have cost the network $3.2 million. Mary remained committed to CBS for one more series, but neither the star nor the network seemed anxious to have that commitment fulfilled; CBS told Mary to take her time coming back, and she indicated that she might take a rather long time. After almost twenty years, it was "lights out" for Mary Tyler Moore at CBS—she would not return for half a decade.

Clearly, in that spring of 1979 the star's brightness was flickering unevenly, and she faced some difficult career decisions. But during the next couple of years, as she battled to rebuild her reputation as an actress, her personal life would once again be torn apart by tragedy and loss. Her reputation would rise phoenixlike from the ashes of her recent failures, but her life would also be changed forever, in unexpected and frightening ways.

12

A Walk
on the Dark Side

Back in February 1977, when Mary was quitting *MTM*, *Esquire* magazine ran a Valentine tribute to her, calling her "America's sweetheart." It consisted of thoughts on Mary from a number of notables. Sounding just like the Rob Petrie of old, Dick Van Dyke said, "She's the best comedienne in the U.S. today. She's so darn good that nonpros don't notice it, but those of us in the business love to watch her." Gloria Steinem said succinctly, "She's shit-free." Nora Ephron, who was soon to write her tale of divorce and romantic angst, *Heartburn*, said, "It meant a lot to me the second time I was single and home alone on Saturday nights to discover that Mary Tyler Moore was at home, too." And Jeane Dixon predicted: "So far we have seen only the budding of her career. Mary will mount to even more scintillating heights and will become one of the first ladies of the American theater."

But the most provocative comment came from Robert Redford, who recalled, "Once while I was renting a house in Malibu, California, I saw her bundled up, walking alone on the beach. I wanted to introduce myself and walk with her, but my respect for other people's privacy prevented it. *The Mary Tyler Moore Show* is the only network show I consistently watch, aside from *Sesame Street*. She seems at once positive, vivacious, vulnerable, attractive, independent, adventurous, and feminine. I would still like to walk with her on the beach." Perhaps it was that image of Mary walking alone on the beach that brought her to Redford's mind a few years later when he read an extraordinary book called *Ordinary People*.

Ordinary People was a publishing phenomenon before it became a successful film. It was the work of a housewife and mother of three in Minneapolis, Judith Guest, who had begun to write when all her children were in school. She had never been published. But she worked doggedly on the book, which tells the story of the Jarretts of Lake Forest, Illinois, one of Chicago's more affluent suburbs. Before the book begins, Cal and Beth Jarrett's older son drowns in a boating accident. His younger brother, Conrad, survives the accident but later attempts to kill himself. *Ordinary People* is about the disintegration of the Jarrett family in the aftermath of these tragedies—the truths they discover about themselves and the destructive and healing power of self-knowledge. Modest in scope, compared to the best-sellers that deal with Ice Age adventures or international intrigue, it was rich in detail, feeling, and characterization. When it was finished, Guest sent it off hopefully to the offices of Viking Press in New York.

It was what is politely called in the publishing industry an "over-the-transom book," meaning that it hadn't been invited by the publisher but simply appeared out of the blue. The less polite but more common name for the hundreds and hundreds of unsolicited manuscripts that publishers receive every year is "the slush-pile." The odds against something from the slush-pile, more than likely by a totally unknown author, ever getting published are astronomically high.

Guest was lucky. The job of plowing through the slush-pile is a thankless one at best, and often delegated to junior members of the editorial staff, or shared out haphazardly among editors who already have more than enough work to do. But *Ordinary People* fell into the hands of Mimi Jones, an earnest editor at Viking. "An English major not long out of college, I was awed and humbled to have this job, and I approached each manuscript with reverence, expecting to have a new *Crime and Punishment* emerge from every Jet-Pak envelope I opened," she recalls. Jones was soon disillusioned, however, particularly when she learned that her supervisor matter-of-factly assumed that all the manuscripts would be rejected. The last time Viking had published a book from the slush-pile was twenty-seven years earlier.

"Still, I kept reading and hoping," she says. "I couldn't help it. And it was true—most of what I read was pretty bad. But one day I unwrapped a novel and started reading, and my pulse quickened. By the time I had finished *Ordinary People*, I was convinced that it was not only publishable, but it was also a book with the potential to touch many people deeply." The novel was serialized in *Redbook*, published to enthusiastic reviews, picked by the Book-of-the-Month

Club, and read by a great many people. One of the people who read it was Redford.

His office reviews a thousand or so scripts, screenplays, books, and other material every year, looking for movie possibilities. What made Redford, then ready to make his debut *behind* the camera as a director, choose *Ordinary People?*

"I wanted to explore some of the elements that had been built up in my life, that were part of my background," he says. "Feelings—how they're dealt with or not deal with in America, the lost community, the idea of change and how necessary it is, and the way the stable parts of our social fabric, the strong and durable things like the family unit, are threatened by change. I remember when I was young, growing up in California, believing that everything was going to be okay. We didn't have much money, but the sun always shone; people seemed to be getting along all right. But I think I felt that there always seemed to be something else. I didn't know what, but something was missing."

Of the Jarretts, Beth is the one who is most threatened by change. Herself an instinctively cold and self-contained person, she fears that too much scrutiny, too much self-examination and brutal honesty, will destroy her family's ability to exist, to tolerate each other. Redford saw in her a chance to develop a theme he had found in his own life.

"The question of appearances versus reality appealed to me partly because I guess I don't see myself the way I appear to other people," he says. "There seems to be an associative set of feelings that go with a person who looks like I do. There have been parts I played that have expressed how I felt inside, but then other times I know my appearance has had a symbolic quality. I've never really felt the way I was supposed to look. As I grew up and traveled, I began to see that people were more concerned with appearance than with how they really were, and when it came down to getting in touch with their feelings, they had to face the fact that maybe they had wasted a lot of their lives. And rather than try to change, they just settled—in their marriages, their jobs. I know it's not always easy to change, but it really depresses me to see someone who I think has chosen to settle rather than face change. That's what *Ordinary People* looks at."

To the surprise of just about everyone, Redford wanted Mary Tyler Moore for the role of Beth. Granted, Beth is attractive, a "perfect" wife, on the surface a sort of Laura Petrie for the eighties. But she emerges as a humorless, unsympathetic character as far removed as it is possible to imagine from the world's image of Mary. But no one dreamed that Redford was hoping to capitalize on the public's surprise or curiosity to build ticket sales—his integrity and his conscientiousness about the film ruled that possibility out. He must have seen a connection that made him believe Mary would work as Beth.

"At first, my desire to cast Mary was purely instinctive," he recalls. "She was the first person who came to mind, visually, when I read the book. I don't know why. The character is so hard to realize, it's such an uphill battle: in order for the character to have some sort of redemption at the end, you have to at least feel something for her. I knew we needed someone you could like in the part, because Beth is likable on the surface. She is, you know, the all-American girl. As to the question of whether Mary could act the part, that was up in the air. I just banked on it."

But while Redford chose Mary in part because he felt she could humanize Beth, perhaps he also saw elements of Beth in Mary. He says, "I remember thinking, 'There's a flip side to Mary Tyler Moore, a dark side,' and how interesting it would be to put that on film. Beth sees herself as a model of self-control, and Mary projects a strong sense of self-control. When she's acting, she's like a Swiss train! She was *terrific* to work with, and, of course, it was very courageous of her to allow that dark part of herself to be used in a major film. She had the guts to accept a very unsympathetic role, knowing her public might expect something much pleasanter from her. In fact, I think she's just about the bravest person I ever met."

Mary, in turn, had total confidence in Redford as director and believes that her confidence was justified. She gave him full credit for helping her create the character of Beth and deliver her performance, lauding the professionalism he displayed in his first directorial attempt. "His demeanor on the set was like it was his tenth film, not his first," she says. "He knew what he was doing, and he knew when he had the take. After he'd gotten what he wanted, he'd let us improvise and add things, like anger, or scratching your knee. His attitude was that of a very secure person. I never saw him lose his temper." He was especially helpful to Mary in helping her watch for and eliminate old, automatic "Mary Richards" moves—elaborate shrugs, twitching shoulders, the trademark grin.

Mary also felt that the movie script, by Alvin Sargent, enabled her to develop the character of Beth successfully. "In the book," she explained, "Beth's an enigma, a shadowy figure, purely and simply the antagonist. In the movie, you begin to understand what made her what she is. You might not like her, but she's comprehensible." Judith Guest later gave Mary a copy of the book with an inscription thanking her for helping to "fill in some of the blanks" in Beth.

"I didn't think of it as courageous for me to play Beth," she adds, "I thought of it as a *great* opportunity for me as an actress." She feels that the "dark side" Redford saw in her was "my ownership of the sad, angry, hostile feelings we *all* have but that some of us take such pains to conceal. I think that Bob, like me, has been a person who's spent his life being pleasant, suppressing thoughts and reactions that might make others uncomfortable or unhappy. He responded to that quality in me." Despite her disclaimer, though, Mary was exceptionally brave in accepting a role that showed her in such a cold, revealing light. That's the paradox of *Ordinary People*. In playing a woman who feared and resisted change, Mary Tyler Moore was facing and even embracing change in her own career. She took a risk on a personal level, too, accepting the possibility that many people who watched Mary force back her emotions and calmly proceed to pack and drive away from her husband and son would say, "Aha—so that's the *real* Mary Tyler Moore coming out at last." Many people *did* respond to Beth that way, and to a certain extent, they were right.

With growing openness and insight (she began seeing another psychiatrist at about this point, and this time she has stayed with him for longer than a year), Mary began to admit the similarities between herself and Beth, saying, "I saw Beth as essentially a strong woman whose main problem was a need to be in command, in control. She comes from the school of 'pull yourself up by your bootstraps.' I think I've been like that from time to time in my life. There are elements of me in Beth. Her strength. The trouble is, she expects everyone around her to live up to that strength. It's her flaw. She sees herself as the perfect picture of order. . . . She can't get in touch with herself, with her feelings." She admitted to harboring greater "depth" and "anger" than the public suspected, and said, "The differences between Beth and me were not as great as the differences between Beth and the characters I'd played before." All of which confirms Redford's initial feeling that Beth Jarrett should be played by Mary Tyler Moore.

But Mary didn't get the part automatically. In fact, she wasn't sure if she'd get it at all. After hearing early in 1979 that Redford was interested in her for the part, she recalls, "I got hold of a script that had been kidnapped—no one was supposed to have one— and I read it and said to my agent, 'Yes, very definitely, I want to meet this man.' Bob set up a meeting in his office, and we had lunch and just discussed Beth—what did I think, what did I feel. He told me what he was going to do with the overall picture. It was really a nice meeting, and I went away and didn't hear from him again for two months.

"During that time," she continues, "I heard through the grapevine that he was testing every actress in town. He called me up once and said, 'I hope you haven't lost interest, because I certainly haven't. I just have some juggling to do in terms of casting. I have in mind certain couplings, but I don't have in mind yet which way I will go.' 'Okay, fine,' I said, 'I can understand it, I can understand it.' And meantime I'm getting tenser and tenser."

Several weeks later, Redford asked Mary to come to his office to meet Donald Sutherland. "I thought, 'Oh, my God, this is going to be the toughest thing in my life, because he's going to be looking at me with a magnifying glass to see whether or not I look right with Donald.' I couldn't stand it," she adds, significantly, "because I had no sense of control, everything was out of my hands. I went to that meeting and everyone sat around chatting about everything from baseball to books and a little about the movie, and then the hairdresser and the wardrobe man came in and we were discussing what kinds of clothes I should wear, and yet when I left the office, he had never yet said, 'I want you to do the film.' "

Mary went from Redford's office to her manager's office that day, and found him on the phone, completing negotiations for the movie deal with Paramount. "It was nerve-racking," she admits, "but the exhilaration when I found out I got it—I didn't think I would experience it again in my life, that feeling that seems to be unique to twenty-year-olds. I identify it with when I used to go and interview for a part and come away four feet off the ground when I got it. It had been so long since I felt that sort of triumph."

Many industry insiders felt that novice director Redford had made a colossal casting error—that perky, sunny Mary Tyler Moore couldn't possibly play the part of a woman who is cold, even cruel, but whose complexity is such that she is ultimately pitiful rather than simply hateful. It was up to Mary and Redford to prove them wrong.

Once Mary was signed, the movie was ready for filming, a ten-week project scheduled to begin in October 1979. But in September, while the casting for *Ordinary People* was still undecided, Mary had agreed to another venture—a return to Broadway in *Whose Life Is It, Anyway?*, replacing Tom Conti, who had to leave the show in October. The play was closed from November until February 1980, when it reopened with Mary as the star. While *Ordinary People* was being edited and prepared for release, Mary was coping with her second extraordinary acting challenge in less than half a year—this time in front of live audiences, something she hadn't faced since *Breakfast at Tiffany's*.

13

WHOSE ROLE IS IT, ANYWAY?

Her decision early in 1979 to return to the stage, if a suitable role became available, is a perfect example of two qualities that have always been prominent in Mary: her bravery (shown by her willingness to try again after her humiliating defeat as Holly Golightly) and her stubbornness (shown by her refusal to let just one defeat stop her). And it's typical of Mary's spunk—that characteristic she endowed Mary Richards with—that she made her comeback attempt not in a light comedy, which might have been supremely easy for her, but in a role that had to be even more demanding than Beth Jarrett. In *Whose Life* she played a quadriplegic hospital patient, totally paralyzed, who sues the hospital for the right to die, and wins—in a role that had been written for and performed by a male actor, award-winning Tom Conti.

Brian Clark, who wrote the play, recalls that the idea of putting a woman in the lead role was first suggested by Jane Asher during the show's London run. Asher, who played the sympathetic physician to Conti's patient, said one night, "How come you get to lie in bed and I've got to prance around the stage

all night? Why don't I lie in bed and you prance?"
Clark considered the idea, and even wrote what he
calls the "British woman's version" of the play; after
all, it's not unheard of for members of an acting
company to trade off roles. In fact, it was standard
practice in Shakespeare's day. But there have been
far fewer cases of women successfully taking on men's
roles (although the great Sarah Bernhardt played not
only Hamlet but Cyrano de Bergerac). For various
reasons, Clark was unable to get the woman's version
produced in London. But when the play opened in
New York, and Conti was required by Actors' Eq-
uity rules to leave after six months, the play's American producer, Manny Azenburg, began to consider
replacing him with a woman.

Michael Lindsay-Hogg, the show's director, says,
"Everyone we approached turned purple at the idea
of a female quadriplegic on stage. They couldn't see
her opting for the right to die the way a man would.
I found that kind of reasoning terribly narrow-minded.
It only made me more adamant to do it." So, when
the various possible male leads failed to work out and
Mary's agent suggested her for the part, she came
under consideration—although Meryl Streep and Mar-
sha Mason were the first actresses approached. Mary
and Grant sat through two of Conti's performances
in one day and "were riveted both times," she reports. She decided that she wanted to try for the
part. She also met with Conti, who prepared her for
the physical difficulties of the role—the challenge of
lying absolutely still, using no movement to express
feeling, and acting with the face and voice alone. He
advised her not to try to recreate Ken Harrison with

a sex change: "he died last October and somehow it just happens that now there's a girl on the horns of the same dilemma."

Once she was accepted, Mary went on to film *Ordinary People* while Clark wrote what he called the "American woman's version," adapting the dialogue to change paralyzed sculptor Ken Harrison into Claire Harrison. "In terms of the number of words, I did more to Americanize it than to transsexualize it," he said, referring to the need to replace "shalls" and "shan'ts" with "wills" and "won'ts." He resisted the urge to change the fundamental tone of the play along with the star's gender. "The whole point for me in doing the play with a woman was to show that this wasn't the tragedy of a man, but the tragedy of a person, that women have sexual needs just as men do, that wit isn't the preserve of males. So to make a lot of changes would have undermined the whole point of doing it at all."

Mary also visited a Los Angeles center for the disabled, where she talked to patients about their disabilities and their dreams. She read the autobiographies of several quadriplegics, trying to understand the emotional storms that wrack their immobile bodies. Once she began learning her lines, she practiced her part in bed at night, lying still and waiting for the itches and twitches to begin so that she could work on controlling and ignoring them. "Poor Tom was always having itches," she said. "That part was easier for me, I think. My training as a dancer helped me to isolate parts of my body."

When the play went into rehearsal, Mary says, she was guided by Lindsay-Hogg to avoid the pitfalls of weakness or sentimentality that audiences might expect a woman to show. He forced her to go for the strongest, most powerful emotional reaction to each scene, rather than relying on her instinct to "play it safe and help the laughs along." Worried that her voice might be too soft or too charming for the character, Mary experimented, finally coming up with a gritty, much deeper voice: "I knew I had to lower my voice several octaves for this role—when I found that voice, the harsh deep voice, I knew I'd found Claire's persona," she told a magazine writer during the run of the play. "Using that gritty voice is killing me. I won't let go of it, though; that's *her*, and I'll stop doing the play before I'll stop using that voice." Despite the fact that her throat hurt constantly (no doubt her chain-smoking habit didn't help), Mary was determined that her audiences wouldn't hear the familiar, girlish voice that used to say "Oh, Mr. Grant" in their living rooms every Saturday night.

Observers were bemused both by the decision to change the character's sex and by the choice of Mary for the part. One critic waspishly wrote, "No part will be safe if the Mary Tyler Moore amendment goes through" and sarcastically suggested future productions of *Hamlet, Princess of Denmark, The Elephant Woman*, and *Death of a Salesperson*. Although he derided the casting decision as pure sensationalism, others were more moderate, and overall the tone was one of "wait and see."

When *Whose Life* opened on February 24, 1980, Mary gave them an eye-opener of a show, one well worth waiting for. "I'm sure many people came to see 'Mary Richards Goes to the Hospital,'" she says.

"But within the first four minutes they were rudely awakened to the fact that that just wasn't going to happen." At the end of the show, Mary received a standing ovation. At the opening-night party at Sardi's, where Conti in a tuxedo and black tie and Mary in a black tuxedo-dress and white tie looked like a photo and its negative, Conti was asked, "Whose life *is* it, Tom?" and unhesitatingly answered, "It's Mary's now." Later Mary admitted that she had been nervous because she knew many people were half expecting her to fail. "I was aware of the ears and the eyes," she told a *New York Times* reporter. "It felt like there was all this pressure in my head, and if someone drilled a little hole, steam would come out. I felt such a great surge of relief and happiness when they all applauded." At last, thirteen years after her first play closed under her, Mary had made it on Broadway.

Although some critics felt that, on the whole, *not enough* changes had been made in the script (one remarked that he found it unlikely that a woman would tell a string of "off-color" jokes or make raunchy remarks to nurses), they were almost unanimous in praising her performance. While recognizing that the play's tone had lost Conti's hard-edged irony, they noted with approval the vulnerability and deep sadness that Mary conveyed. The *Times* called her performance "accomplished and finally quite moving." *Time* magazine said: "Without taking a single step, she has made the transition from TV to the stage in perfect stride."

Mary also received accolades from her friends— which meant as much to her or as the praise of the critics, maybe more. Robert Redford came backstage after her first performance to congratulate her, and Ed Asner sent her favorite telegram: "Nice to know all those dancing lessons have paid off at last." She was also touched and pleased by the encouragement of the general public. "People here in New York, the theater crowd, are so responsive and nice and pleased for your success," she said marveling. "I hear 'Hey, we saw it last night and it's wonderful!' or 'We're coming tonight!' Everyone on the block is pulling for you." Not everyone—Mary did receive several anonymous death threats from cranks during the show's run.

There was only one dissenting voice in the chorus of good reviews. John Simon panned the show and especially Mary. "Oooh, that man!" Mary said after reading his review. "He just ripped me to pieces emotionally. He hated me, he thought I was just dreadful. I don't remember the words, but I'll carry the pain around forever." What particularly enraged her was Simon's blatant sexism. "Can you believe that Simon couldn't understand why Claire Harrison would want to die because her sex life was over? He could understand a man's wanting to die if he were deprived of sex. God almighty! How *dare* anybody deny a woman's sexuality, how *dare* anybody imply that women are only the passive recipients of sex? Women enjoy sex, are aggressors at times—why in heaven's name not? I hope you are taking notes," she instructed her interviewer. "I want you to say that I am now stamping in fury!"

Simon's misguided diatribe aside, however, Mary basked in the knowledge that she had pulled off an astonishing coup. But simply having proved that she could act the part well wasn't enough. She also had to keep doing it, day in, day out. This was a new learning experience for Mary, after years of TV and movie work. *Breakfast at Tiffany's*, of course, didn't count. "We played the thing such a short while that I never understood the problems of *duplicating*, eight times a week, the spontaneity that a stage performance should have every time," she says. But she adds, "It was the most exciting thing I've ever done, working night after night in front of a live audience."

At first in *Whose Life*, Mary was afraid to take chances. "I played it very safe, because in the theater you have no second chance, as you do with taped TV or film. God, there's no *editing*. You've only got that two-hour moment in which to be wonderful!" she explains. But as she gained confidence, she began to enjoy the challenge of keeping her performance fresh week after week. The discipline required was unremitting. "I'm amazed at how inert I'm able to be onstage," she said then. "I expected lots of uncontrollable twitches and itches. I had a muscle spasm during one emotional scene—a killer spasm that I thought would do me in. It didn't. Fear of ruining the play overwhelmed any urge I had to relieve that physical pain. I just gritted my teeth and lived through it. If my nose itches, I tell myself, 'This is just a nose itch, it will go away, don't panic.' And it does go away. . . . Wouldn't it be awful to think this wasn't great acting, this was just overcoming a nose itch?"

A week after the show opened, *Variety* reported that, despite good press, ticket sales were slower than had been expected. Although the same article pointed out that "it's generally agreed in the trade that her portrayal is emotionally involving and exceptionally accomplished . . . a textbook example of a star from another medium rising to the artistic challenge of legit performance," the suggestion was made that perhaps TV and movie stars were finding it tough to draw Broadway audiences. That same season, film stars Richard Gere, Mia Farrow, and Roy Scheider were doing poor box-office business in *Bent*, *Romantic Comedy*, and *Betrayal*, respectively. But there was speculation that if business picked up, Mary might extend her original six-week contract. She did so, and played the part for 14 weeks.

When the Tony Awards rolled around in the spring of 1980, everyone spoke of Mary as a hot contender for best actress. Because of a technicality, however, she was disqualified, having replaced another actor in the role rather than opening in it. But she was not to go home from the awards ceremony empty-handed. In a surprise move by the presenters, she received a special award for her "bravery" in taking on the role of Claire and her overall contribution to the theater season. While most onlookers agreed that she deserved it, the award bent a few noses out of shape in the theatrical community. One belonged to Isabelle Stevenson, president of the American Theater Wing, who objected that the award had not been put to a formal vote and the honor was therefore "fuzzy." But this tempest in a teacup fizzled out quickly and Mary was left in possession of the award, which she had certainly earned. Another dazzling triumph awaited.

Ordinary People premiered in mid-1980, to glowing reviews. Everything and everyone received high praise:

Redford as director; Timothy Hutton's sensitive but strong performance as the tormented Conrad Jarrett; Donald Sutherland, as the middle-aged husband and father trying desperately to meet his family's conflicting needs (and his own); Judd Hirsch, as the unobtrusively caring psychiatrist—and Mary, as the chilled-steel Beth. The depth and fineness of her portrayal won notice from every reviewer. She was described as "remarkably fine, simultaneously delicate and tough and desperate" in the *New York Times*, and other newspapers and magazines were equally complimentary. Inevitably, there was a certain amount of surprise that the Sunshine Girl could so convincingly play the Ice Queen, coupled with hints that there might well be more to Moore than met the eye. But the overall reaction was enthusiastically positive, and the words "Academy Award" began to be heard when *Ordinary People* and Mary Tyler Moore were mentioned. On top of her success in *Whose Life*, the movie's reception made Mary feel like a trillion dollars, at least.

She had become all too familiar with headlines like "Mary Tyler Moore Flops Again" during the previous few years. Now it was time for her to relax and enjoy the height of her professional prestige. But the dramatic downturns of her personal life during 1980 more than wiped out any hope of Mary having a good year.

"YOU'RE GONNA MAKE IT AFTER ALL . . ."

On October 14, while movie audiences everywhere watched Beth Jarrett icily repudiate her suicidal teen-age son, Richie Meeker shot himself fatally in the head at his home in Los Angeles. He was twenty-four years old.

The circumstances were uncannily close to those of Elizabeth Moore's death two years earlier. Like Elizabeth, Richie was involved in a troubled love af-fair; like her, he was something of a stranger to Mary; his death, like hers, hovered somewhere in the gray area between accident and suicide. They were even close together in age. But Richie was Mary's son, and his loss was deeper, more intimate, and more painful for her.

Mary learned of Richie's death, as she had learned of Elizabeth's, from Grant. She was in New York, where Grant reached her after he had received a call from Detective Jerry Ferrin of the Los Angeles Police Department. Ferrin also told Grant that the death would be listed as "accident or possible suicide" until the circumstances had been fully investigated.

The shooting took place at eleven-ten at night, in

the rented house Richie shared with two women friends, both students. One of them, Judy Vasquez, was in his room while he played with the .410-gauge shotgun he kept hanging on the wall near his bed. (Friends say he had bought the gun to shoot rabbits; one report said that he had bought it as protection against burglars; but his father, who probably knew best, said simply, "He liked guns. He had them all over the place.") The other roommate, Janet McLaughlin, had gone to her room to study.

According to Vasquez's account, Richie had just finished talking on the telephone to his girlfriend, twenty-one-year-old Linda Jason of Fresno. While he chatted with Vasquez, he sat in lotus position and placed the butt of the gun on his ankles, pointing at his face. He began loading and unloading a shell, clicking the chamber each time, and playing a gruesome combination of Russian roulette and "she-loves-me, she-loves-me-not," using the shotgun instead of a daisy. "She loves me." Click. "She loves me not." He stared at Vasquez and shouted, "She loves me!" and the blast from the gun blew into his face. The sound of the shot and Vasquez's screams brought McLaughlin, and the two girls ran screaming to the neighbors for help. An ambulance was summoned and rushed Richie to a hospital, but he was pronounced dead twenty minutes after the shooting.

Mary, Grant, and the three young women involved were quick to assure the police and the press that the death was accidental. One of Richie's roommates said that the gun was defective. Grant said, "Both Mary and I had talked to him that day. He was never more 'up.' " And his girlfriend, Linda Jason, said, "I know it

wasn't suicide. He was the happiest he's ever been."
Police investigators weren't so certain, however, and
it wasn't until January of the following year that the
county medical examiner's office ruled the death a
suicide. But the tormenting questions must have remained in Mary's mind: What *really* happened? How
could Richie, who knew all about guns, have allowed
such an "accident" to happen? And would a young
man who was really happy with his life, who harbored no self-destructive urges, have played the ma-
cabre game with death?

It was inevitable that the tragic similarity between
the death of Mary's real son and her movie son's
suicide attempt should catch the fancy of reporters
and headline writers. But Grant insisted on Mary's
behalf, "The movie has absolutely nothing to do with
this. There are no parallels." It was just, as everyone
connected with Richie insisted, a grisly coincidence.
But the result was to make Richie's death even more
newsworthy than celebrity tragedies usually are. Mary
must have been torn between grief and anger to see
tabloids shrieking: "Life Imitates Art as Star's Son
Slays Self." Sadly, her sorrow was deepened still
further by the fact that after years of estrangement,
she and Richie were finally learning to like each
other.

They had gone through a period of severe alienation during Richie's teens and early twenties. He
had chosen to live with his father, and there were
long periods when he and Mary didn't communicate
at all. But in the year or so before his death, Richie
and Mary's relationship had mellowed. They talked
more frequently, especially after Richie, who worked

as a messenger in the CBS mailroom, decided that he wanted to be an actor. Although he refused to let Grant and Mary help him, he did share his excitement over landing a part on *The Dukes of Hazzard* (unfortunately, the actors' strike intervened and the segment was never filmed). In fact, Mary's public-relations manager says that Richie's career was the subject of her conversation with him on the evening he died.

Ironically, one symbol of the improving relations of mother and son was the California preview of *Ordinary People*, which Richie attended with Mary. A few weeks earlier, Mary had told a reporter that she had drawn on memories of raising Richie to portray Beth's relationship to Conrad in the movie. "I was kind of a perfectionist mother and I demanded a lot of him. I think I was responsible for a lot of alienation—although we've since become very close," she said. "So I brought some of that to the part and enlarged it and magnified it." She added that one of her first steps in preparing for the part was to review the script with her psychiatrist. "I asked him if it could be true that a woman can't express her feelings for her son."

Mary had also mentioned one of the movie's most painful, wrenching scenes: Conrad, hoping to bridge the growing gap between himself and his mother, puts his arms around her and kisses her. She stiffens, her hands flutter like frightened birds, and tears glisten in her eyes. When asked why Beth doesn't kiss him in return, Mary said sadly, "She wanted to, but she can't get by that iron encasement." She added that during the filming of the scene, "I was thinking of Richie."

Now, after his death, she said of Richie, "In the last year and a half he had really gotten himself together, was a responsible person, had developed self-respect. Richie had grown up. He was becoming my friend."

Richie's funeral was a ghastly ordeal. Mary wept throughout the service. Richie was cremated and his ashes scattered in the Sierra Mountains. Friends and well-wishers did what they could to help her through the crisis: Dick Van Dyke called Mary at least once every day, and Ed Asner "just held me in his arms and sobbed half the night through with me," she recalls. A taped interview with Rona Barrett that was scheduled to be broadcast right after Richie's death was canceled at Mary's tearful request. Jimmy Carter, Billy Graham, Frank Sinatra, and others sent condolences. And Mary says that what helped her endure the aftermath of the funeral was answering these letters: "I sat down and wrote a thank-you note to every single person who'd written to me when Richie died. It took many days, and I was sorry when there were no more letters to answer. I got through those terrible months and the devastating sense of loss with friends who cared, who made me laugh, who have a history with me."

Mary's sorrow over Richie's death was complicated by the fact that she was facing it alone. Mary had been in New York when Richie died because she was now living in an apartment there. She and Grant had separated formally in December 1979, as Mary was finishing *Ordinary People* and preparing to open in *Whose Life*.

"The separation is best for both of us," Mary announced to the press. "We have very positive feelings about each other and are sure we're doing the right thing. We will remain close but not married." Characteristically, the taciturn Grant's comment was more terse: "We're packing it in." Both claimed that they had tried for some time to avoid taking this step, but that it was inevitable. And both claimed that while they were sure there would be no reconciliation this time, they had no definite plans to divorce.

Grant and Mary continued to be business associates; he helped her arrange the deals for *Ordinary People* and *Whose Life*, and, naturally, they were partners in MTM Enterprises. But Grant left his post at MTM to work for NBC, and Mary hired a film scout and began to make moves toward developing projects of her own. She also began to make many changes in her life—some of them difficult ones.

First, though, she forced herself to carry out an activity she had been involved in at the time of Richie's death: promoting *Ordinary People* for an Academy Award. She kept busy, lunching with Redford, granting interviews, being seen and photogrpahed around town with friends, including Warren Beatty. Mary's refusal to curtail her professional and social activities may be interpreted as an act either of coldness and insensitivity or of rigorous self-control and a need to occupy her mind and her time. Given her distress at Richie's funeral and the sadness she has shared over losing him, it is impossible to believe that she did not feel his death deeply and for a long time.

It is much more likely that her frantic activity in the months after his death was a form of therapy.

Ordinary People had won the New York Film Critics Circle vote as best film of the year—usually a sign that it was a likely Oscar winner. It was nominated in the best picture category and, to her delight, Mary was nominated for best actress. Her competitors was Ellen Burstyn for *Resurrection*, Sissy Spacek for *Coal Miner's Daughter*, Gena Rowlands for *Gloria*, and Goldie Hawn for *Private Benjamin*. It was generally agreed that Hawn and Spacek—whose films had been huge commercial successes as well as artistic ones—were the two to beat.

On March 31, Mary showed up at the awards ceremony, clad in a dazzling off-one-shoulder gown and a broad smile for her first television appearance since Richie's death. She was on hand not just in the event that she received her award but also as a presenter, for the best supporting actor category. One of the nominees was Timothy Hutton, for his role as her son in *Ordinary People*. In an emotional moment that carried a sense of half-fearful tension, he ran to the stage to receive the award from Mary— and they hugged each other. But she had to call on another kind of bravery later in the evening, to keep smiling when she was passed over as best actress. Sissy Spacek, who had played a warm, loving character that audiences couldn't help but admire and love, copped the Oscar.

Mary may not have received an award for *Ordinary People*, but she was proud of the film. One of her fondest memories is of the night in New York, shortly after it opened, when she happened to be in a car that stopped in front of the theater where the movie was playing. "I couldn't believe it!" she remembers. "I saw *two* long lines, one for that showing and one for *advance* tickets. I asked the driver to stop a moment. I cried. I was so proud—it was like being proud of my own kid!"

Back in New York, Mary spent the next six months doing something she had never had to do before—designing a brand-new, solitary life for herself. With a vision sharpened by the highs and lows of the past several years and by her sessions with the psychiatrist she called "my professional friend," she started to look back on her life, her relationships, and her marriage. And for the first time, her obsessive need for personal privacy diminished a little. She granted scores of interviews, in which she talked freely about the direction her life had taken. It was as though, in discovering things about herself for the first time, she had to share them.

One thing she examined was her failed marriage. She acknowledged that Grant had been the dominant partner—and for the first time, she admitted that she had been unhappy with that situation. "It's chauvinistic for men to think that they are the more important members of the family," she said, adding a remark that revealed a new degree of self-awareness: "Our relationship was that of a father to a child." But she also defended Grant—and herself—from the oft-repeated charge that he directed her career, saying, "He didn't make my career choices—I'd never have allowed that, even if he were so inclined, which he wasn't. I do still rely heavily on Grant's opinion, I always will. I send him scripts even now." But Mary's dependence on Grant's professional help was to decrease further over the next couple of years, as he left MTM to work for NBC, where he is now chairman.

Shortly before their separation, Mary had said that she would never accept a project that would take her away from Grant for any period of time—she said that she'd be "desperately unhappy" without him. After the split, it seemed that the remark was not the expression of devotion it had appeared to be, but rather an ominous foreshadowing of what she must have known the future held in store. "Sure, I said that," she says. "Some things you say to convince yourself. When I said I was happy with Grant I was aware of our problems—we both were. But—especially when you're questioned—you tend to stress the positive side and to assume things have a chance of working out. You do believe the good at the time, you want to believe it, it's not a lie. Of course, you come to a point where you can't kid yourself or others anymore, and you act.

"Grant and I made the decision to separate together," she goes on, "after long, long talks analyzing our lives." But she refuses to give any details about what precipitated it. Grant, on his part, is equally uncommunicative, saying only, "It's a very private matter. What Mary chooses to say of it is her business. She's a big girl, very big in every good sense of the word. We had seventeen terrific years together. Why does a marriage break down? It simply . . . runs out of gas." It's interesting that Grant, in talking about Mary, automatically uses phrases more appropriate to a father talking about his little girl—even after the separation.

In December 1981, Mary was in California again, filming her next movie—her first work since Richie's death. She was able to stay in the huge Bel Air house, with the sixty-by-forty-foot ballet studio, that she and Grant had built together not long ago; he was living elsewhere. Soon after, he bought the house from her. She was thrilled that he would be keeping the house he had helped design. She left most of their furniture and belongings there for him, and even let him keep the dogs and all the needlepoint pillows she had compulsively made over the years, saying that they didn't belong in her New York apartment.

Six Weeks, with Dudley Moore (no relation to Mary), was a turkey of a movie that bombed at the box office. It paired Mary, a high-powered cosmetics-company queen, with Dudley, a politician on the rise; the relationship was engineered by her daughter, who is dying of leukemia and has only six weeks to live. The movie's sickly sentimentality and the depressing death scene in a subway turned audiences off, but the film is worth noting on several counts. First, it continues the pattern Mary had developed of interest in projects involving illness or disease: Betty Rollin's cancer in *First, You Cry*, Claire Harrison's paralysis in *Whose Life*, and Beth Jarrett's emotional disorders in *Ordinary People*. Soon she would take on still another medical subject, heart disease, in a TV movie. At this point in her life and career, Mary seemed to need to control her own fear of illness by mastering it, or at least confronting it, on the screen. Her health appeared good, but she was suffering from problems about which the general public wasn't to learn for several years. But the specters of disease and death could be faced down in fiction, if not in real life.

It's also touching that *Six Weeks* portrayed the death of Mary's child, played by a young ballerina, Katherine Healy. Because of their shared interest in dance, the two became close and even worked out together during the filming. Getting to know Katherine may have sparked Mary's present-day feeling that it would have been good to have a daughter. She says of their on-camera relationship, "It has a closeness unlike most mother-and-daughter relationships. She was very mature for her age—we are almost contemporaries; we are each other's best friends." And it's clear that she is remembering Richie when she adds, "Most parents and children don't become friends until the child grows up." Just before his death she had said that she had found "a new friend" in him.

After *Six Weeks*, Mary returned to New York and a period of concentrated work on a different kind of project: her domestic life. She had been subletting the small East Side apartment of art dealer Marjorie Reed, but was in the process of decorating and moving into the apartment she had purchased in a 1930s building on the Upper West Side, overlooking Central Park. Candice Bergen had recommended decorator Angelo Donghia, and Mary spent nearly a year working with him to remodel and design her new home. The result was featured in a special article in *Architectural Digest*, and Mary admits it's something different for her.

The homes she had shared with Grant had been comfortable and expensive, but not terribly stylish or distinguished. Their interiors had favored warm, cozy chintz, dark wood furniture, an English or French country look. But Donghia told her, "You're making a major change in your life. It's time to leave all that behind and do something new." Mary agreed, not without some trepidation, and together they created a luxurious, yet subdued set of rooms. The colors are netural, the fabrics and materials opulent but unobtrusive, the effect elegant. Special touches include antique ebony doors to the dining room, recessed shelves to house Mary's collection of scripts, Emmys, and memorabilia, and a small collection of pre-Columbian American Indian figurines. But there are a few touches of the old country French look as well. "We made some compromises," Mary says, "softened a few edges here and there. We took an old French armoire and bleached it, so it's not all modern. *Something*'s left of my old life." But the overall effect of the apartment is of a new life.

Another new element Mary explored was friendship. Her friendships had always been slow growing and a little superficial, and for many years Grant had been just about the only person in her life. "It's wonderfully easy to make friends here!" she exclaimed after a year in New York—a far cry from the way she'd hated the city when she lived there briefly in 1966. But although she said that living in New York was opening her up to new friendships, the truth is probably that the difference was in *her*, not in where she lived. She was receptive to overtures. "Hope Lange just called me up the other day," she announced, marveling. "I don't even know her. She said, 'You're in town alone, I'm in town alone, let's have brunch.' " They did—possibly sharing anecdotes about starring opposite Dick Van Dyke, which Lange did after Mary—and became good friends. Mary made other women friends, too, including photographer Brigitte Lacombe ("who's been sharing with me some of the joy there is in being single, also the disappointments") and publicist Pat Newcomb ("the first to shake me by the shoulders and say, 'You've got to start initiating things, don't wait for them to come to you' ").

She also learned how to spend time alone, which wasn't easy for someone with a compulsive need to be busy. She learned to relax, to judge herself less harshly, to make the most of life on her own. As she put it, "I'm learning at age forty-four what most people learn at age twenty-two." She had never really been on her own before: she'd married at seventeen, been single for only three months between marriages (and those three months she spent living with her mother and grandmother), and since then had only been alone for six weeks, during her first separation from Grant. This was new and unfamiliar territory. As she put it, she had to "work through the real mind-and-body shock that after all these years of marriage, I'm on my own, making my own decisions— this after a lifetime of being with strong men, beginning with my father. Men had made my major decisions, and I had allowed it. Now I have to take charge of my own life. Sometimes I'm optimistic, sometimes pessimistic. I think, 'What am I doing? I might make a mistake.' But one thing I learned: mistakes don't end the world. It just goes right on with you or without you, and you learn from your mistakes." Clearly, Mary brought not only courage but also wisdom to the challenges of her new situation.

The irony of her situation was not lost on her. After seven years of playing America's premiere single girl on TV—years during which she'd been married and very sheltered—suddenly Mary Tyler Moore was living Mary Richards's life. "It wasn't until I was in my forties and living on my own in New York that I learned what it was like to be a single woman," she says. "I kept remembering the episodes of the show that dealt with the problems of a single woman— being lonely, having disastrous dates. In three years I went through almost every one of the experiences that I could only guess about when I played the role."

She remembers one day in particular when this realization was brought home to her while she was sitting outside her psychiatrist's office smoking a cigarette: "They were playing that elevator Muzak. I was feeling a little depressed that day and, don't you know, over the Muzak they started to play the theme from *Mary Tyler Moore*. You know, 'How will you make it on your own, girl? *How will you make it on your own?*' I laughed. I wanted to stop people who were walking by and say, 'Do you realize what is happening?' "

As fans of the show will remember, the final line of that old theme song is a joyous affirmation: "You're gonna make it after all!"

15

SOMETHING
TO SMILE ABOUT

Mary said more than once after their separation that although she and Grant would not attempt a reconciliation, they would not divorce: "This separation is amicable but final. We just haven't divorced because we don't see the need unless we wanted to marry other people. But neither of us is ever going to marry again. That's what Grant says of himself, and I know it's true of me." But she was careful to add that she wouldn't rule out the possibility of having a long-term relationship with a man, living together. "I just don't see the need for marriage unless you plan to have children," she would say, and then with the next breath, "Grant's my dear, good friend and always will be. The act of divorcing him just seems *unfriendly*, a hostile thing." But the couple eventually agreed that there was no reason for their marriage to continue, so in late 1981 they "pushed the button," as she puts it, and were divorced.

As if to prove that the marriage was indeeed over and that Mary Tyler Moore was starting over, she had already embarked on a dating spree and was obviously enjoying it. She was romantically linked at various times with Michael Lindsay-Hogg, her director in *Whose Life;* with writer Pete Hamill; with Warren Beatty ("just friends," was Mary's comment); with Steve Martin, who squired her to the premiere of *Six Weeks;* with millionaire bon vivant Sir Gordon White, who made something of a hobby of actresses—at one time or another his collection had included Marilyn Monroe, Rita Hayworth, Grace Kelly, Susan Hayward, and Jane Russell, so Mary was in exalted company; with public-relations man Ed Menken.

Some of these "romances" were simply media or PR fabrications, such as Warren Beatty and Steve Martin. The important ones were Sir Gordon White, whom Mary dated and discoed with in New York, Paris, and England during the summer and fall of 1981, and Ed Menken, who came into her life in 1982. Mary and Ed vacationed together in Europe, but she laughingly insists that it was innocent, even accidental. According to her, she planned to take her parents on a trip to Europe that October, and they wanted very much to meet the Pope. Mary's show-business clout didn't mean a thing in the Vatican, but Ed was connected with Daytop Village, an organization to fight drug abuse among children, and through this connection was able to arrange an audience. Then, Mary says, "he had to come to Rome on business and wound up staying in the same hotel—that's all!" Nevertheless, the tabloids had a field day with their relationship.

In view of Mary's feelings about the Church, it is perhaps surprising that her audience with the Pope moved her so much. She says it was a "transcendent," a "supreme" experience. "I thought I was perfectly calm," she recalls. "But I was wearing a big black hat, and I happened to look up, and the hat brim was trembling." Mary reacted to the Pope not as the symbol of a religion she had long ago abandoned, but as a charismatic, overwhelming human presence. The audience Ed Menken had arranged was the high point of the trip. But Ed soon faded out of the picture.

Curiously, it was the trip to Europe that led to the next important relationship in Mary's life—the one that was to turn her life on its head again. When she returned from Europe, Mary's mother, Marjorie, who was staying with Mary in New York, was ill with bronchitis, and Mary insisted that she see her doctor. But Mary's doctor was at Yom Kippur services when she called, and she was referred to a stand-in: a Dr. S. Robert Levine, a cardiologist at Mount Sinai Hospital in Manhattan. He agreed to see Marjorie at once.

Robert's friends and colleagues, while leery of violating his privacy by discussing his relationship with Mary, have said that he is a warm, caring, responsive man, easy to talk to and easy to like, as well as a brilliant and conscientious physician. All of these qualities were apparent to both Mary and her mother as soon as they met him. Something else was apparent to Mary, too. This young—*very* young, in fact, only twenty-nine years old—doctor was also attractive: tall, dark-haired, and handsome. "Shame on you, Mary, you naughty girl," she recalls thinking. "He's too young for you." But when the young doctor gave Mary his home number and told her to call in case of emergency, she joked, "Does acute loneliness count?" He said yes.

A few nights later, Mary dialed the number. "I knew I wanted to see him again," she says. "I felt there was definitely chemistry between us, but I thought he might be too intimidated by my public image to pursue it, so I did—at about two in the morning! I was feeling very brave when I made that phone call!" Mary Richards and Rhoda Morgenstern, if they had been there to look over her shoulder, would have been proud of her.

Mary remembers that first conversation well. She said, "Do you cook?" He said, "No, I don't." She said, "Neither do I, so I guess we'd better go out to dinner." They had dinner together the next night, and soon they were dating steadily. "I wasn't looking to fall in love," Mary says. "You'd *know* I wasn't looking if you saw my apartment in New York. It's beautiful—but small! I spent a year redecorating it with the idea—the certainty—that I'd be living there alone for the rest of my life." But although she didn't begin the relationship with the intention of getting serious, Mary's feelings changed rapidly. "I had thought this would never happen to me again," she says. "But my feet were not quite touching the floor—they were just skimming it. And what happened to my appetite? Why couldn't I read this book? I'd been staring at the same page for an hour." She also says, "My love for Robert evolved quickly. It started as a strong attraction to a wonderful guy, and before I knew it I was a little in love, and then I was lot in love, and then I was married!" The marriage took place on Thanksgiving eve, November 1983, at New

York's Pierre Hotel. Three hundred family members and friends attended the Jewish ceremony. Mary was forty-five and Robert was thirty.

Mary was aware that her decision to marry a much younger man would give rise to much comment and speculation, but she wisely chose to disregard it. She and Robert discussed the issue carefully and decided it was what they truly wanted. "We're both rather traditional people, actually," confesses the woman who swore she'd never marry again.

Certain catty columnists suggested that Mary had begun dating Robert to even the score with Grant, now fifty-seven, who was frequently seen with Melanie Burke, a secretary in her twenties who looked startlingly like the young Mary. One source claiming to be a friend of Mary's said that Robert would have made a better affair than a marriage, and another called him "a big bore." Other friends, including Valerie Harper, who was a bridesmaid, were delighted for Mary and fond of Robert; Harper and Hope Lange were among the guests at a bridal shower, where Mary received such joke gifts as a stethoscope and sexy lingerie intended to induce house calls. On the eve of their wedding, Grant Tinker sent the couple an orchid plant, with a note saying, "Be sure you keep this alive."

Predictably, most of the public remarks about the marriage centered on the age difference. What with Olivia Newton-John, Joan Collins, and many others leading the way, it's not all that unusual anymore for a woman to marry a younger man, particularly if she's a successful, confident woman with the inner strength to defy convention. But society still looks askance at such marriages, according to New York psychologist Penelope Russianoff (she played Jill Clayburgh's therapist in *An Unmarried Woman*): "People say, 'She's robbing the cradle' and 'He's marrying his mother,' and that's rotten," she says. It seems possible, however, that there is a tiny element of truth in these clichés, no matter that Robert and Mary are truly in love. Mary, having recognized the pattern of her earlier marriages, says, "For the first time, I haven't married my father. This is an equal marriage, not fifty-fifty but one hundred–one hundred." Perhaps, in ensuring that she wouldn't marry another father figure, Mary subconsciously went in the opposite direction and fell in love with a son-substitute. Robert is only two years older than Richie would be. Unlike Richie, though, he's a grown-up, professional adult who knows what he wants—and it happens to be Mary. She says he has decided that children and a family aren't important to him—although, she adds scrupulously, "he could still have them someday. I could die, and he could remarry. But the fact that we won't have a family doesn't bother him."

Oddly enough, Mary had once considered the hypothetical possibility of getting involved with a younger man, long before she met Robert. In February 1981, she told a writer for *Cosmopolitan*, "*I* don't think of a man's age at all. I've been with men—no, I don't want to say who—who are a lot younger than me but who make me feel quite naive and immature. . . . I think of myself as being too young, in terms of experience. Otherwise, I won't let age be a limitation." Maybe Mary felt that her relative lack of experience and Robert's relative lack of years matched them up nicely.

As for the other difference between them—her fame and his anonymity—it hasn't bothered either of them, she claims. "The very first time we went out, we were walking along and suddenly Robert stopped in his tracks," she says, "and he said, 'What am I doing here walking down the street with Mary Tyler Moore?' And that was the last time it came up." His approach to some of the more trying burdens of fame is also refreshingly relaxed. One day Mary tearfully showed him a tabloid that had printed a sensationalistic, distorted story about him. She expected him to be angry and upset, but he just laughed and said, "That? It's just a silly pack of lies. Why worry about it?"

One of the gifts Robert has brought Mary is that he's helped her to feel and show affection in a relaxed way. "I've become a toucher and a hugger. I never used to be that way," says she. "It's influenced my work, too. In a key scene with Jim Garner in *Heartsounds* I found myself touching him, something I wouldn't have done a year before." She also appreciates Robert's thoughtfulness, which he shows in small, inventive ways. Once when she was in Washington on business, for example, Mary ordered scrambled eggs for breakfast from room service. But when she lifted the cover from the dish, she found that it contained her favorite breakfast, a fried toast-and-egg concoction that Robert had introduced her to. "Robert had called the chef that morning and said, 'No matter what she's ordered, here's what to do.' Then he gave him the recipe over the phone. Now *that's* thoughtful."

Every now and then, Mary says, she'll be reminded of the fifteen-year difference in their ages, "When we're watching an old movie and Robert will ask, 'Who is that?' And I'll say, 'Esther Williams.' And he'll ask, 'What did she do?' Then I'll say to myself, 'Hmmmmm.' But that's superficial. What matters is we have fun together and enjoy each other. I just live for now. If Robert and I have five wonderful years together, or ten or twenty—whatever—then our decision to marry has been a very wise and good one."

Love and marriage weren't the only things happening in Mary's life in the early 1980s. She was also involved in two film productions and plans for a return to television. She also caught the world off guard with the headline-grabbing revelation of yet another dent in the saintly image of the old Mary Tyler Moore: alcoholism.

16

New Beginnings

Mary, more relaxed and at ease with herself than ever before in her life, enjoyed her new marital status so much that for a few months she was content to stick close to home with Robert. She decided to screen possible new projects carefully, rejecting those that might take her away from home for too long, and settle on something she really wanted to do. In the spring of 1984, she had found it.

Martha Weinman Lear's book *Heartsounds* was the true story of her husband's battle with heart disease. During the course of a heart operation, Hal Lear, himself a doctor, suffered brain damage that caused the quality of his life—and of the Lears' marriage—to deteriorate between the operation and his death. Noted TV producer Norman Lear had been Hal Lear's cousin and was to produce a TV movie based on the book for ABC. Director Glenn Jordan wanted to use comic actors in the key roles, if possible, hoping to repeat the formula he had used in *Only When I Laugh*, a potentially depressing story of an alcoholic's recovery. His idea was to use James Garner—fresh from his success in Blake Edwards's *Victor/Victoria*—as Hal

Lear and Mary Tyler Moore as Martha. Mary agreed to do the project, which would be filmed partly on location in Manhattan and partly in Toronto, fast becoming a mecca for U.S. filmmakers because of its relative affordability.

Although Robert could not be with Mary in Toronto throughout the filming, of course, he did visit on weekends and took an interest in the activity on the set. On the six-month anniversary of their marriage, he had her dressing-room trailer filled with six huge bouquets, one for each month.

A source inside the production company reveals that the years haven't dimmed Mary's perfectionism, her insistence on having the script meet her notions of what is right—or her determination to be a star. She is said to have ordered a rewrite because she thought the original gave too much emphasis to Garner's part and not enough to hers. The final version involved more than 250 scenes and was a complicated and trying movie to film. Mary may have had some reservations about working with Garner, who had a reputation for irascibility and feistiness; he was suing Universal Studios, for example, for more than $22 million, allegedly owed him in residuals for *The Rockford Files*. If so, her fears were groundless. Over the course of the filming, a comfortable, bantering relationship developed between the two stars. Mary would nag him affectionately, he would grumble about it good-naturedly. Director Jordan had banked on the two having what he called "a community of rhythm, a fund of experiences to bind them" from their long years on television, although they had never before worked together. His hunch played off, and the pro-

duction was noted for its touching blend of tragedy
with warm domestic realism, even humor. It was
broadcast in September 1984 and reviewed moderately
well. Mary received kudos for allowing herself to
portray an older, even plainer woman than she had
ever before done on TV; she had not permitted vanity
about her appearance to compromise the movie's
realism.

Heartsounds completes a sort of progression in Mary's
choice of roles dealing with the somber subjects of
disease and death. *First, You Cry* and *Whose Life* had
allowed her to play seriously or fatally ill characters;
Ordinary People had given her an emotional, rather
than a physical, sickness to portray; *Six Weeks* imposed the painful task of watching her child sicken
and die. Now *Heartsounds* gave her a dying husband.
But there was a difference. Not only was the illness
in this movie outside Mary's own character, as it
had been in *Six Weeks*, but the movie was not an
absolute tragedy. Like the book, it sounded a strong
note of hope and affirmation, stressing the durability
of love and human relationships in the face of mortal-
ity. It suggests that Mary's obsession with the theme
of death has finally been resolved with understanding
and acceptance.

As soon as work was completed on *Heartsounds*,
Mary commenced her next project, another film, which
for reasons of logistics and availability had to be done
back-to-back with *Heartsounds*. Called *Finnegan Begin
Again*, it was filmed in Virgina in six weeks during
late summer. After her serious roles of the past half-
dozen years, it was a welcome return to comedy, a
touching and funny story of improbable love. It was

also an intriguing reversal of her own real-life love story with Robert—possibly her experience with him is what interested Mary in the story. Mary played a young-to-early-middle-aged widow who was having an unsatisfactory affair with a mortician, played by Sam Waterston—his gifts were bouquets pirated from funerals; their outings were morticians' conventions. She meets a much older man, a disillusioned journalist with an invalid wife, and gradually, tenderly, they fall in love. Although both Burt Lancaster and Jason Robards turned down the role of Mary's older swain, it was played to perfection by Robert Preston. Like Garner, Preston had scored with the hit *Victor/Victoria*, where he had shared a bed with Julie Andrews—as her gay friend Toddy. He said smugly of his role as Finnegan: "There's actually a sacking-out scene. I get to make love to Mary on the floor in front of a roaring fire. Now what other sixty-six-year-old gets a chance like that?"

Once again, though, Mary felt that the script needed work before she was satisfied. She held a week-long session of rewrites, rehearsals, and conferences before the filming began. Even during the shooting, she occasionally suggested changes. One such suggestion resulted in a brilliantly funny scene: the script called for Waterston and Preston to slug it out over Mary in a cemetery. At one point, Waterston was supposed to fall into an empty, muddy grave. Mary felt that the scene might work if *she* fell in, too. The director agreed, and Mary, immaculately coiffed and dressed, urged the crew: "Please, let's try and get it in one take," then plunged into the mud. The movie was shown on the Home Box Office cable network in

February 1985 to excellent reviews. Although not a mass-market crowd pleaser like *Ghostbusters*, it offered wit, charm, and polished performances to those viewers who were ready for a little romance. And it pleased Mary that Robert, who visited the set on weekends, took a tiny part: "I think there's a performer in there trying to get out," she says of him fondly.

At the same time that *Heartsounds* was hinting to network audiences that she may have come to grips with her fear of illness, Mary took a bold step in her personal life, confronting one of her own demons head-on. She entered the Betty Ford Center in Rancho Mirage, California, for treatment of alcoholism in October 1984.

Again, as with so many of her moves during the past few years, the press dredged up the old image of perky Mary Richards and reacted to the news with shock and amazement. Once more, Mary Tyler Moore was admitting that she wasn't perfect . . . just human.

The Betty Ford Center is part of the Eisenhower Medical Center about ten miles outside of Palm Springs. Three recovering alcoholics—a doctor, tire tycoon Leonard Firestone, and former First Lady Betty Ford—established it in 1982 as a source of treatment for drug and alcohol dependency. Most of the Center's patients are ordinary, upper-middle-class folks—only about one percent of them are celebrities. But it is the treatment of stars like Liz Taylor, Tony Curtis, Liza Minnelli, and Robert Mitchum for which the Center is most famous. The treatment program is rigorous—based on a "tough love" approach that doesn't fool around when it comes to confronting patients with the truth about themselves—and egalitarian, with no special privileges for celebrities. The success rate is about 75 percent.

Because so many of the Center's patients, especially the highly publicized Hollywood stars, suffer from drug as well as alcohol problems, Mary and Robert were at great pains from the outset to announce that Mary's problem was with drinking, period. They also stressed that her drinking was not excessive—at least, it would not be excessive for a nondiabetic. Her condition, however, made the use of *any* alcohol dangerous. And she had been drinking for so long that she was unable to stop on her own.

Mary had had dizzy spells and episodes of weakness during the hectic summer, and Robert had drawn blood samples and charted her blood-sugar rate for two weeks, even waking her at night to make his tests. His conclusion: alcohol and her body chemistry didn't mix. "It's expected to drink in the social and business circles in which she moves," he said. "But it was my feeling, shared by her doctors, that drinking was dangerous to her. She's at Betty Ford because her doctors and I thought she needed a supportive environment for abstinence. Her goal is to gain some strength and understanding that it's okay to say no to alcohol." He added, "I'm a bit of a martinet on health matters." He himself drinks only occasionally.

Mary gives Robert credit for helping her make the decision to stop drinking. "I want to describe accurately the kind of alcoholism I suffered from," she now says. "It was a controlled alcoholism, but nevertheless a full-blown case of it. Nobody ever saw me drunk, and in fact I wonder if I ever *was* drunk—but it had a hold on me, it was an important part of my life. It was the way in the evening I let go of all the control I'd exercised during the day. . . . At a certain time of day I'd sit there with my 'best friend'—my cocktail—whether I was happily married or alone." She also began to suffer from memory lapses, which she called "terrifying."

In response to the observation that the Betty Ford Center has become an "in" place to be seen, Mary says, "Do you really think anybody would court all that pain just to be trendy? My God!" But the pain was worth it—Mary has stopped drinking. Robert makes it clear that she will have to control her desire for alcohol and her diet forever "to survive to a normal age." With his support, she is trying—successfully, so far—to kick another lifelong habit, smoking. Late in 1985 she suffered a hemorrhage behind her right eye from a condition known as diabetic retinopathy, which can cause blood vessels in diabetics to burst. Smoking aggravates the condition. Says Mary, "If the doctors hadn't told me that it was 90 percent sure I'd go blind if I didn't stop, I'd probably still be smoking—rationalizing my way through. God, I loved every one of those cigarettes I smoked. Smoking was a buffer—a way of not connecting with people." Mary seems to need fewer buffers these days. Now she gets by with an occasional piece of sugar-free bubble gum.

Mary made another new beginning in December 1985 when she returned to series television for the first time in six years. *Mary*, which premiered on December 11 on CBS, is a half-hour comedy very much like the old *Mary Tyler Moore*. Mary's back in

the newsroom, but this time she works at a decidedly
yellow tabloid, the *Chicago Eagle*, which features such
stories as "Arsonist Sets Self on Fire—Wedding Night
Spoiled." (Just before the series was set to begin,
MTM lawyers found to their dismay that the name
they had originally chosen for Mary's paper, the
Chicago Post, belonged to a small neighborhood paper
published by a local politician in Chicago. He threatened to sue, saying, "I wonder what they would
think if I used the MTM logo on a can of dog food,"
and the technical wizards at MTM did some last-
minute splicing and dubbing to change the paper's
name in the segments already filmed.)

Mary's character, Mary Brenner, is a lot like an
older, slightly sharper-edged, hipper Mary Richards—a
Mary Richards for the eighties. And this time around,
fifteen years after CBS executives vetoed the idea,
she's divorced. She's still childless, however. She's
surrounded by a colorful crew of colleagues, she has
a comfortable, classy single-woman's apartment, she
has a zany girlfriend. In the third episode, she even
threw a terrible party. If it sounds familiar, it's because it *is* familiar. With few changes, Mary has
returned consciously to the character and setting she
did best in television. After her disastrous variety-
show flops, she may simply have wanted to play it
safe.

It's likely, too, that Mary felt an urge to update her
most famous character, to add the elements of her
own life that she has acquired in the post-*MTM*
years: a divorce, a weekly group therapy session with
women friends, a tougher, less diffident, and more
direct approach to humor which is very attractive.

It's also interesting that her new series contains one element that the old one noticeably lacked—an ongoing romantic tension, which never quite takes the form of action, with a series regular. He's her boss, well played by James Farentino, and their teasing, love-hate relationship seems modeled on those currently popular in *Moonlighting* and *Remington Steele*.

Although CBS was committed to purchasing thirteen episodes of *Mary*, it remains to be seen whether the series will survive. Early ratings were disappointing—but then, *Mary* has taken off after slow starts before. Ironically, one of the casualties of the 1984–85 season was a sitcom called *Sara*, starring Geena Davis as a single career woman. Billed as "the *Mary Tyler Moore* of the eighties," it bombed. Maybe the upwardly mobile, predominantly female, predominantly twenty-five-to-forty-year-old audience that it was aimed at were too busy working out at their health clubs and attending wine tastings to watch *Sara*, but *Mary* may be able to lure them back to the screen.

She'll be seen on the big screen, too, in a film called *Something in Common*. Starring Ted Danson (of *Cheers*) and Christine Lahti, it's about a friendship between two women that is threatened when one of them has an affair with the husband of the other. It was written for Mary by Allan Burns, who helped create Mary Richards.

Mary says that she can't imagine ever not working— "it would be like not breathing." She expects to go on acting, playing older and older parts in a wide variety of stories. She has come a long way from the dancing pixie and the faceless pair of legs. She's an acclaimed, talented performer and a power in the world of show business. She has arrived at an understanding of her strengths and weaknesses that should help her stay successful as her career continues. Out of disappointment and grief, she has forged self-knowledge and new beginnings. She has a new life and a new love. The famous smile is older, less ingenuous, but none the less radiant, as is the woman. For now, it seems, she's on top of the world again.

And as much as she likes to be in control, Mary admits that she doesn't know what the future holds for her. Whatever happens, though, one thing is certain: Mary Tyler Moore will still be smiling. She's a survivor.

About the Author

Rebecca Stefoff is a Philadelphia-based author and journalist. She has interviewed scores of people, from the famous to the non-famous, for such publications as *The National Star*, *The National Enquirer* and *Good Housekeeping*. She is a contributing editor on subjects from health and nutrition to personalities for a magazine called TLC, which is distributed to patients in hospitals. She has written seven books, including two gothic romances and three health books.